About the Author

Clark M. Eichelberger was one of a committee of five who prepared the first American working draft of the UN Charter. In 1945 he acted as a consultant to the U.S. delegation at the San Francisco Conference. He devotes much time to writing and lecturing about the UN, was Executive Director of the American Association for the United Nations and is now Vice President of the United Nations Association.

UN: THE FIRST TWENTY YEARS

UN

THE FIRST TWENTY YEARS

CLARK M. EICHELBERGER

HARPER & ROW, PUBLISHERS
NEW YORK

LIBRARY OF CONGRESS CATALOG CARD NUMBER: 65-14650

To the memory
of President and Mrs. Franklin D. Roosevelt

CONTENTS

FOREWORD

The United Nations is twenty years old. These years are not comparable to a fraction of a second in the millions of years of evolution it took to produce man nor in the thousands of years of his recorded history.

Why, then, are the past twenty years of United Nations' history so important? Why, then, do we place so much store on the next twenty years of its history? In previous ages life moved slowly. Generation followed generation, with little change in their mode of living. Several generations of men created the great cathedrals in the Middle Ages.

Now, for the first time in history, man has the capacity totally to destroy himself and his fellows. Scientists warn that in the extreme an atomic war could destroy the physical conditions from which man evolved; never again could this earth produce man as we know him, with his dreams, his aspirations, and his efforts to approach his God.

At the least, an atomic war would so destroy the fabric of modern society that man would be reduced to anarchy, isolated groups struggling to find a living from a contaminated earth.

However, man's capacity of destruction is matched by his capacity to save himself. In so doing, he would build an infinitely better world.

That is why the last twenty years and the next twenty years assume greater importance than some centuries in the history of man's development. There will be other great crises in man's long future. There will be great changes in his continuous life on this planet. But if there is to be that future, our task in this generation is to rid ourselves of the war system. Man must have an organized society because all of his future depends upon his being able to live peaceably.

The twenty years' history of the United Nations family would take volumes to do it justice. I have tried, therefore, with a few broad strokes, to show how much has been accomplished in twenty years' development of the United Nations. I have tried to show where it has fallen short and how much must be done in the near future to strengthen it.

It is not by accident that the Charter of the United Nations begins with the phrase, "We the peoples of the United Nations . . ." instead of beginning with the phrase of the League of Nations Covenant, "The high contracting parties. . . ." In the final analysis, it is up to the statesmen and the people they represent to make a success of the United Nations. I should like in this book to make an appeal to people, not to fall back, or to permit their statesmen to fall back, into the traditional ways of thinking about world diplomacy and power. Rather I should appeal to them boldly to devote themselves to carrying into practical life the purposes and the principles of the United Nations Charter.

In the preparation of this book I am indebted to so many people that I shall not try to enumerate them. I am indebted to many friends in the United Nations field. I am indebted to many officers of the United Nations Association and the Commission to Study the Organization of Peace for sharing ideas. And I am particularly indebted to members of the staff of the Association who have made valuable suggestions for the improvement of the manuscript as well as giving invaluable assistance in its technical preparation.

UN: THE FIRST TWENTY YEARS

I

INTRODUCTION

The two decades during which the United Nations has been in existence have seen scientific, political, and economic changes that stamp them as comprising one of the great revolutionary periods of history. The United Nations has been the deciding factor in helping the world survive these changes, and in so doing it has been profoundly changed. The interpretation of the Charter and the machinery itself are vastly different than contemplated at San Francisco when the Charter was drafted.

The Scientific Revolution

The first decade after the Second World War witnessed the beginning of the atomic age. The second decade can be identified with the beginning of interplanetary travel. The statesmen who were drafting the Charter at San Francisco were unaware that atomic bombs were about to be dropped, ending the war quickly. They could not have been aware that there would be a scientific development that would profoundly change the security calculations upon which the Charter was based.

Scarcely had the nations reconciled themselves to the atomic age when another horizon was penetrated—the horizon of outer space. The latter may present the world with even greater possibilities for adventure and more profound decisions than has atomic energy.

Undoubtedly the world is on the threshold of further scientific advancement. Of all the scientists that the world has known through its thousands of years of recorded history, 90 per cent are alive today. The organized society of nations must grow accordingly if the world is to have peace.

What steps have been taken in the United Nations to meet the challenge of the scientific revolution, what steps are contemplated, and indeed what steps will be necessary as far as one can foretell will appear in succeeding chapters.

The Human Revolution

Comparable to the scientific revolution has been the human revolution; indeed, they have had an effect upon each other.

1. The Revolt of Colonial Peoples

Over seven hundred million people, more than one-third the world's population, have thrown off the yoke of colonialism since the Second World War began. Freedom has come to a large part of Africa, the last extensive bastion of colonialism, at a rate no one would have imagined when this author's book *UN: The First Ten Years* was written. Indeed, as the second decade of the United Nations ends, only a few scattered peoples are without self-government. Less than 2 per cent of the world's population now lives under colonial rule.

The rapidity of this development was not anticipated at San Francisco, although its seeds were planted in the organization. The Charter of the United Nations has become a charter of liberty under which colonial peoples aspire for freedom. The organization itself, particularly the General Assembly and the Trusteeship Council, has provided the forums in which appeals for freedom can be made. Now, one-third of the membership of the United Nations is made up of new states. They have made a profound change in the power balance of the organization.

Nothing better illustrates the achievement of freedom in the colonial world than the fact that the United Nations buildings are already crowded. The General Assembly Hall was built to accommodate seventy delegations, which was the anticipated membership of the organization in our time. The Assembly Hall has been done over to accommodate one hundred twenty-five, which is the anticipated membership in a few years. The Trusteeship Council room has been converted into another large committee room because so rapidly are the trust areas being freed that the Trusteeship Council becomes smaller and may not be necessary a few years from now.

2. The Revolt Against Misery

The revolt against hunger and misery has accompanied the revolt against colonialism. Half the people of the world are hungry. Many of them cannot read or write. The life expectancy of some of them is not more than thirty years. A large percentage of them have a per capita income of less than one hundred dollars a year. Some of these people have rich and ancient cultures but are up a blind alley economically. Others are so primitive that they have not discovered the use of the wheel. A great restlessness is sweeping over the underprivileged peoples. It is not necessary for them always to be miserable, and they do not intend to be so.

The last twenty years have witnessed the population explosion. If it continues, seven billion people will inhabit the earth by the end of the century. The increasing food production has not done much more than keep up with the growing population.

Assuming that the danger of war is put far into the background, disarmament advanced, and colonial peoples freed, the problem of helping the underprivileged part of the human race achieve a better life under conditions of democracy and freedom will remain the most absorbing problem of the United Nations. Over half of the budget of the United Nations family is devoted to this problem.

Breakup of the Five-Power System

Another change that the United Nations has had to survive, to adjust to, and if possible to turn to good account, has been the breakup of the five-power system accompanied by the creeping paralysis of the cold war.

The late U.S. Secretary of State Edward R. Stettinius, Jr., in presenting the United Nations Charter to the Senate Foreign Relations Committee in 1945, explained that giving the five Great Powers permanent seats and the veto in the Security Council was simply recognizing the power facts of life. The United Nations, he said, would depend for its success upon the unanimity of these five. Others referred to them as the world's policemen, who would keep order for years to come.

It was a miscalculation in 1945 to assume that the five Great Powers would remain united. It was a mistake to assume that the increasing membership of the United Nations would be content with the domination of five. Indeed, the Charter could not in 1945 determine which nations would be the five Great Powers in the indefinite future. However, had the cold war not set in, the Great Powers could have been united on major problems during the reconstruction period. Had these powers remained united, the world would be a much happier place. Thousands of lives lost in local conflicts, a constant stream of refugees, the poisonous invective that has assailed the ears, would have been avoided.

How the United Nations developed to overcome the

breakup of the five-power system runs like a thread through this entire narrative.

UN: The Decisive Factor for Peace

The last twenty years have been years of unparalleled change, danger, defeat, and bold adventure. Scientific horizons have been penetrated. A great part of the world has won its political independence. An effort is being made to provide a society of abundance for all mankind.

At the same time, many efforts at improvement were chilled by the paralyzing effect of Communism, which, at least for the first ten years after the war, continues to expand. The problem was made even more difficult by the fact that the Soviet Union made the first foray into outer space.

What has kept the peace in these fantastic years? The Marshall Plan? It saved the West from bankruptcy. NATO? It may well have saved Western Europe from invasion. The Organization of American States? Certainly it continued to keep the protective mantle of the Monroe Doctrine around the nations of the southern part of the Western Hemisphere. The Baghdad Pact and the Eisenhower Doctrine? Their beneficial effects are questionable. The nuclear stalemate? Here is the peace of fear, for each side in the bipolarized world knows that an initiative on its part would be met by instant retaliation and the destruction of all.

However, the decisive factor for world peace has been the United Nations. It has made the difference between the uneasy peace in which the world has lived and a third world war. Every day since the Second World War ended there has been spasmodic fighting somewhere on earth, but these conflicts have not resulted in a third world war. The United Nations has made the difference. It is hard to define the many specific and subtle influences of the United Nations on the

side of peace. One phrase, however, may best describe it—
"moral unity."

Suppose the nations had entered the atomic age in a world
of anarchy. The author knows from interviews with the late
President Franklin D. Roosevelt that he feared a repetition
of the reaction of 1920 that kept the United States out of the
League of Nations. He was determined that at least a provisional United Nations be created before the fighting ended.

What if the United Nations' allies had not carried out
President Roosevelt's intention? What if the nations had not
formally adopted principles of good conduct with laws
against war? Suppose they had not created a common meeting place, with machinery for the peaceful settlement of disputes? Suppose they had not provided a forum in which the
peoples dominated by colonialism could petition peacefully
for their freedom? Suppose the newly created United Nations
and Specialized Agencies had not set in motion a process for
the relief of economic and social misery? If these things had
not been done, it is doubtful that the world would have survived this long. The changes in the postwar period were so
great and so terrible in their potential for destruction that
without the unifying force of the United Nations the world
might well have destroyed itself.

So far the United Nations has survived one defiance after
another, one neglect after another, and has seemingly
emerged stronger than ever. Nations may ignore it for a moment, but usually return to it as the only means to meet
world problems.

As the third decade of the United Nations opens, one hundred fourteen nations are bound by the obligations of the
Charter. More will be so bound in the next few years. The
peace of the world is dependent upon their becoming increasingly integrated into an international society by the
many bonds that the United Nations provides. It is essential

that the moral unity be strengthened every day by devotion and common usage.

The ever-present danger is that the member nations may fragmentize their concerns by alliances and bilateral action, that they may lose the vision of world society. It was so in 1955, in 1960, and it is true in 1965. The United Nations has passed through repeated crises, some of them so serious that commentators predicted the death of the organization. The fourteenth year of the United Nations (1959) closed with the Secretary-General reporting to the Fourteenth General Assembly: "The past year has been characterized by intense diplomatic activities mainly outside the United Nations although in some cases within its precincts or in informal contact with the Organization." The Security Council had had only five meetings in that entire year. There were no emergency meetings of the General Assembly.

The tragic collapse of the Summit Conference between President Eisenhower and Chairman Khrushchev in May, 1960, ended these particular bilateral negotiations outside of the United Nations. The problems of the Congo brought the major attention of the world back to the Security Council.

The United Nations begins its twentieth year with problems equally serious or even more so than those of the previous years. The refusal of some nations to pay their special assessments for United Nations peacekeeping forces threatens the organization with bankruptcy. The African states are in danger of permitting racial hatred to blind them to obligations that they assume as members of the organization. War is raging in the Indochinese peninsula without having been brought to the attention of the United Nations as the Charter obligates. The NATO powers seemingly see no inconsistency in discussing a multilateral nuclear force while the General Assembly and the Geneva Disarmament Conference discuss ways to stop the proliferation of nuclear weapons.

The world will have peace if the sense of moral unity imposed on the nations by the Charter and the habits of cooperation developed in nineteen years are strong enough to prevail against the forces of fragmentation. The history of the last nineteen years would justify one in believing that the present crisis, too, will pass and the United Nations will emerge with greater physical and moral strength.

II

PEACEFUL SETTLEMENT AND COLLECTIVE SECURITY

The purpose of the United Nations is to prevent war.

The United Nations was born in the tragedy of the Second World War. While the framers of the Charter were meeting in San Francisco, Allied forces were fighting beyond the German frontier and the forces in the Pacific were island-hopping before the assault on Japan could begin. The Charter begins by stating that the peoples of the world are combining their efforts to accomplish certain objectives. Understandably, the first objective was "to save succeeding generations from the scourge of war, which twice in our lifetime has brought untold sorrow to mankind. . . ."

Because they were aware that conflict began with the violation of human rights in Germany and Italy, the framers of the Charter declared as the next objective: "to reaffirm faith in fundamental human rights, in the dignity and worth of the human person, in the equal rights of men and women and of nations large and small. . . ."

In the third paragraph the framers addressed themselves to the political and legal side and determined "to establish conditions under which justice and respect for the obligations arising from treaties and other sources of international law can be maintained. . . ."

And finally, looking forward to the prospect of a better life when the scourge of war was removed, they wrote as a fourth objective: "to promote social progress and better standards of life in larger freedom."

There is a fine logic in the sequence of these four objectives. The first and third are based on the prevention of war and the establishment of peaceful processes. The second and fourth reaffirm faith in human rights and social progress. They look toward the removal of the basic causes of war and anticipate a better way of life, in which war would be thought of less and less.

The total purpose, then, of the United Nations is the maintenance of peace. The over-all method by which it is to be accomplished is the development of a dynamic international society in which nations are held together by many visible and intangible bonds of civilized adjustment and development. As man develops the means of total destruction and the capacity to explore celestial bodies, the scope of the dynamic international society must continue to grow. He dreams of an order in which nations will be so enmeshed in cooperative peaceful efforts that serious political disputes would seldom arise and the threat of war would be unthinkable.

The purpose of this book is to portray what progress has been made in twenty years to achieve these aims. Where have the efforts fallen short?

The peaceful and just society requires civilized methods of adjustment. The United Nations increasingly provides them. These methods may be of various kinds, including debates in the General Assembly or informal conferences in the Delegates Lounge at headquarters. Various technical conferences include scientists, doctors, businessmen, labor leaders, university professors, and farmers. Constant contact in many areas of human living set the climate and method of adjustment and provide an atmosphere of permanence. Out of these agreements come custom and habit that contribute to the development of world common law.

At times, when the problems of adjustment become sharper, they enter the realm of political disputes that must be settled and of imminent or actual aggression that must be prevented or stopped.

This chapter will deal specifically with the work of the United Nations in settling disputes that might lead to conflict and in preventing or stopping aggression.

The Charter suggests that the nations first of all attempt to settle disputes directly. It suggests a variety of means for dealing with them. Article 33 of the Charter states: "The parties to any dispute, the continuance of which is likely to endanger the maintenance of international peace and security, shall, first of all, seek a solution by negotiation, enquiry, mediation, conciliation, arbitration, judicial settlement, resort to regional agencies or arrangements, or other peaceful means of their own choice."

However, in using any of the above methods the nations cannot escape the obligations of the Charter. They cannot threaten force to accomplish their diplomatic objectives. And if the nations fail to settle directly disputes that constitute a threat to the peace of the world, they are obligated to bring them to the Security Council. They should not delay such submission indefinitely, as has been done in the case of the fighting in Vietnam.

Machinery for Peaceful Settlement and Enforcement

Back of the wide variety of direct methods of adjustment is presumed to be the firm hand of the Security Council, ready to act under Chapter VI of the Charter. This hand becomes firmer as that body moves from Chapter VI to Chapter VII, which gives it authority to act to prevent or stop aggression. Chapter VI and Chapter VII outline the methods and obligations for the peaceful settlement of disputes and also how aggression shall be prevented or stopped. Chapter VI is entitled "Pacific Settlement of Disputes." Chapter VII is entitled "Action with Respect to Threats to the Peace, Breaches of the Peace, and Acts of Aggression."

Under Chapter VI, the Security Council may investigate any dispute or any situation in order to determine whether their continuance is likely to endanger the maintenance of international peace and security. The Security Council may recommend appropriate procedures or methods of adjustment. However, if the situation becomes worse, the Security Council can then move to Chapter VII, under which it "shall determine the existence of any threat to the peace, breach of the peace or act of aggression and shall make recommendations, or decide what measures shall be taken in accordance with Articles 41 and 42, to maintain or restore international peace and security."

In order to prevent any aggravation of the situation, the Security Council may recommend or decide upon provisional measures that nations must live up to and carry out while an effort is being made to solve the problem. Article 41 provides that the Council "may decide what measures not involving the use of armed force are to be employed to give effect to its decisions. It may call upon the Members of the United Nations to apply such measures. These may include complete or partial interruption of economic relations and of rail, sea, air, postal, telegraphic, radio, and other means of communication, and the severance of diplomatic relations."

But should such methods not be enough, the Security Council may then really get tough. Under Article 42, it "may take such action by air, sea, or land forces as may be necessary to maintain or restore international peace and security. Such action may include demonstrations, blockade, and other operations by air, sea, or land forces of Members of the United Nations."

There is a logical progression in the Charter, beginning with Chapter VI (for the peaceful settlement of disputes) through Chapter VII (providing for the use of military force to stop aggression). However, there is much difference between theory and practice. Later it will be seen how much of the work of the United Nations to prevent or stop conflict has been a pragmatic approach without being rooted specifically in these clauses of the Charter.

Three bodies of the United Nations—if one may refer to the Secretary-General as a body—bear the major responsibility for carrying out the provisions of the Charter relating to international peace and security.

The Security Council, according to the Charter, has the "primary responsibility for the maintenance of international peace and security." As far as the United Nations is concerned, it has certain sovereign powers. The members agree that it acts in their behalf and that they will carry out its decisions. They will maintain armed forces to be at its command. The use of such authority, however, is contingent on the Great Powers acting unanimously—something they have seldom been able to do.

The Security Council also has a built-in summit conference, which has never been used. Under Article 28 (2) "The Security Council shall hold periodic meetings at which each of its members may, if it so desires, be represented by a member of the government or by some other specially designated representative."

In comparison, the General Assembly is concerned with the entire range of United Nations activities. These include the development of economic and social cooperation, human rights, international law, and the entire housekeeping operations of the organization.

While the Assembly has competence in the fields of peace and security, its authority is much less precise than that of the

Security Council. True, the General Assembly "may discuss any questions relating to the maintenance of international peace and security brought before it by any Member of the United Nations. . . ." It may "recommend measures for the peaceful adjustment of any situation, regardless of origin, which it deems likely to impair the general welfare or friendly relations among nations. . . ." It is limited, however, in that it must abstain from making recommendations on any matters with which the Security Council is dealing. In other words, the framers intended that in the area of peace and security the Security Council could command, the General Assembly could recommend.

The General Assembly, in the words of the late Senator Arthur Vandenberg, was to be a "town meeting," ranging over the whole field of international problems and making recommendations regarding them.

The Security Council is weighted in favor of the five Great Powers because each has a permanent seat and the right of veto. The General Assembly is weighted in favor of the small states because each regardless of size has one vote.

The Secretary-General is the Chief Administrative Officer. He shall perform such functions as may be entrusted to him by the major organs of the United Nations. "The Secretary-General may bring to the attention of the Security Council any matter which in his opinion may threaten the maintenance of international peace and security."

The preceding paragraphs have described the authority and competence of the Security Council, the General Assembly, and the Secretary-General—that is, as defined in the Charter. If the United Nations had been held to a literal interpretation of these provisions, the organization would have exploded. A shift in the relative authority of these bodies, their interplay, the development of unanticipated means for the settlement of disputes, and the development of legislative and executive functions in the General Assembly comprise one of the most fascinating and dramatic parts of the United Nations story. It is still unfolding.

The previous chapter referred to the breakup of the five-power system. This fact has had a profound effect on the relationship of the Security Council and the General Assembly. From the beginning, the Great Powers demonstrated that they would not be united much of the time. Part of the time the Security Council has been paralyzed by this lack of unity, expressed in sterile cold-war debates, in over one hundred vetoes of the Soviet Union, and in one case by the vetoes of France and the United Kingdom. All the Great Powers, with no exception, have at times seemed more interested in scoring points against their opponent in the cold war than in reaching an agreement on the merits of the problem.

Wherever the chilling efforts of the cold war were absent, the Security Council had a chance to function as was intended. However, as the cold war extended to one geographic area after another, the influence of the Security Council was reduced proportionately. The cold war finally reached the Middle East. In the early days, the Soviet Union supported the establishment of the State of Israel. Today, a Soviet vote on the side of the Arab states in any Middle East dispute with Israel is considered automatic.

Aside from a lack of Great Power unity, there were other reasons for the development of the General Assembly as the dynamic body of the United Nations. The Charter provides that the nonpermanent members of the Security Council shall be selected with due regard paid ". . . in the first instance to the contribution of Members of the United Nations to the maintenance of international peace and security and to the other purposes of the Organization, and also to equitable geographical distribution." These criteria have frequently been overlooked. Consequently, the many new and small powers with little chance to be represented on the Security Council were increasingly anxious to bring political disputes to the General Assembly.

Many of the disputes call for the processes of peaceful change. Walter Lippmann, writing in the New York *Herald Tribune,* said: "The common factor in all three situations is that they are the aftermath of the breakdown of the old imperial systems—the French system in Indochina, the British system in the eastern Mediterranean, and the Belgian system in central Africa."

The necessity for peaceful change also accounts for the growing dynamism of the General Assembly. The Security Council is set up to deal primarily with threats to the peace or situations whose continuance might lead to a threat to the peace. It seldom looks ahead. It acts when confronted by a crisis, usually brought to it by one of the parties to a dispute. It is the General Assembly, however, that must deal with the problems and challenges of a developing world; these run all the way from the liquidation of the colonial system to the potential threat of spaceships carrying atomic weapons. Consequently, what the Assembly does in its deliberations and its resolutions tends to have a binding effect not originally anticipated. They add to world common law.

It is fortunate for the peace of the world that the Charter has been liberally interpreted. Instead of being a strait jacket, it has become the means for unanticipated approaches to the problems of peaceful change, of peace and war.

The most spectacular example of a liberal interpretation of the Charter occurred with the adoption of the Uniting for Peace Resolution. It provides that if the Security Council, because of lack of unanimity of its five permanent members, fails to act on an apparent threat to the peace, breach of the peace, or act of aggression, the Assembly itself may take up the matter within twenty-four hours—in emergency special session—and recommend collective measures, including, in the case of a breach of the peace or act of aggression, the use of armed force.

The work of the Secretary-General has expanded. U Thant has said: "The role of the Secretariat, and of its Chief Administrative Officer, the Secretary-General, has also developed in response to the challenges which the Organization has been called upon to meet. The office of the Secretary-General, in particular, has been found to be a useful place for the mediation and conciliation of disputes and for informal diplomacy and exchanges of views, while at times the Secretary-General has been called upon to assume executive functions, especially in relation to peacekeeping operations. . . ."

As the years have gone on, the roles of the Security Council, the General Assembly, and the Secretary-General have tended to be intertwined in dealing with the problems of war and peace. It is almost impossible to describe to any great extent the work of one body or of the Secretary-General without discussing the others. There are times when the three cooperate to achieve a result. Even when the Security Council acts without the General Assembly, the latter body has been responsible for the financing that makes the work of the Security Council possible. And the Secretary-General, as the Chief Administrative Officer of the United Nations, is called upon to implement the decisions of these bodies.

The Security Council has a record of important decisions that have prevented war. Any critical meeting is widely attended by the public and widely reported. Representatives of many countries watch the deliberations, hoping with all their hearts that the eleven men around the horseshoe table will be able to make decisions and enforce them. The public feels that these eleven men, with proper authority from their governments and with courage in their hearts, can make important decisions. And these decisions can be backed by a strength of action authorized by provisions of the Charter.

Any critical meeting of the General Assembly is also widely attended and widely reported. The General Assembly is a reflection of the world as it is. Are the peoples of the world capable of meeting their problems? Here one sees developing a parliament of mankind in which the nations are seeking means to deal with the overwhelming problems of peaceful change within the framework of law and parliamentary procedure.

New Methods to Deal with New Problems

In meeting these many disputes and threatening situations, the United Nations has developed a variety of methods that have not been spelled out in the Charter. It has established various commissions for truce supervision. Forty UN military observers in the mountain passes of Kashmir are maintaining peace between the Pakistani and Indian forces. The United Nations has a Truce Supervision Organization reporting on the observance of the four general armistice agreements concluded by Israel with Egypt, Lebanon, Jordan, and Syria. It maintains approximately one hundred twenty UN military observers along Israel's frontiers.

The United Nations has established agencies for the control of subversive border crossings. In 1946 the Security Council established a Committee of Investigation to report on the border difficulties between Greece and her neighbors. When the cold war prevented the Council from reconsidering this situation, the General Assembly established an eleven-member United Nations Special Committee on the Balkans. Its purpose was to report on the implementation of the General Assembly resolution calling upon Albania, Bulgaria, and Yugoslavia to stop all aid to Communist guerillas.

In 1958, Lebanon charged that an internal revolt was being fomented by outside elements crossing its borders. The

Security Council established a United Nations Observation Group in Lebanon to report on illegal crossings. While the body was not able to uncover much evidence, the presence of impartial observers would seem to have contributed to the restoration of peace in that area. The Group's final report said that it had been "a symbol of the concern of the international community for the welfare and security of Lebanon," and that by "helping to free the Lebanese situation from its external complications, [the Group] has contributed to the creation of conditions under which the Lebanese people themselves could arrive at a peaceful solution of their internal problems."

The Security Council provided for the appointment of a Good Offices Committee to assist in settling the political dispute between the Netherlands and the Indonesian Republic. Dr. Frank Graham ably represented the United States.

For some months the United Nations exercised all of the authority of a state in administering West Irian (formerly West New Guinea) in the transfer from Dutch to provisional Indonesian sovereignty.

The United Nations exercised a more extensive sovereign role in building a state out of the surrendered Italian territory of Libya.

An altogether new concept in United Nations language is the United Nations "presence." When Jordan felt herself menaced by her neighbors, the Secretary-General sent one man, to be known as the United Nations "presence" in Jordan. This single man, or "presence," without any military force at his command, was the symbol of the moral and the legal force of the community of nations as expressed by the United Nations. Tensions lessened. Although his office is in Geneva, he is still considered the United Nations presence in Jordan.

Regretfully, the United Nations presence that originally

had something to do with reducing the threat of war between Thailand and Cambodia was withdrawn because Thailand indicated that it did not favor continuing the mission on a permanent basis.

It is impossible to describe in detail every dispute with which the United Nations has had to deal, or to describe every situation aired in the Security Council or the General Assembly. When the President of the Security Council convened the body on December 30, 1964, he said: "The 1,188th session of the Security Council will please come to order." With the exception of the sessions devoted to completing its annual report and dealing with the question of membership, most of these meetings were primarily concerned with trying to resolve disputes that were a threat to world peace. A report issued by the Secretary-General in early 1964 listed sixty-two matters of which the Security Council is "seized"—meaning matters on the docket because they have not yet been cleared up or removed.

In addition to these Security Council meetings, the General Assembly has had eight extraordinary or special sessions that in the main have dealt with disputes brought to it under the Uniting for Peace Resolution, when the Security Council had been unable to act because of a Great Power veto. It would be impossible to analyze all the disputes dealt with by these bodies of the United Nations. Consequently, it would seem best to describe several of the major problems that have given the United Nations the greatest concern—the greatest fear of war. They are also disputes in which the United Nations has charted new ways, has added to its experiences, and has contributed to the common law of nations.

Korea and Collective Security

First, Korea presents a clear example of United Nations application of collective security.

In the ideal state of international society, the United Nations would be able to mobilize forces to prevent or stop aggression. The Charter of the United Nations provides such procedures in Chapter VII. The powers of the Security Council and the obligations of the members to carry out its instructions have already been dealt with.

From the establishment of the League of Nations to date, the possibility of organized resistance to aggression has been called collective security. Collective security involves certain legal procedures previously agreed to. There must be a legally constituted international body capable of passing judgment on the facts of aggression based on previously accepted law. Following the determination of such facts, a legally constituted body must not only authorize but order resistance to aggression. The members of the world society must accept the obligation to resist aggression regionally or universally if called upon. And finally, it is assumed that there must be a collective force, potential or in being, that can be used to stop aggression. These elements for collective security are to be found in the United Nations Charter.

United Nations resistance to aggression at the 38th Parallel in Korea, undertaken on the initiative of the United States, was history's most nearly complete example of collective security. The facts of aggression were certified to by an agency of the United Nations. This certification was so complete that when the Security Council met on June 25, 1950, to consider the aggression, no nation dared ask for a delay on the excuse that the facts were not known.

This was a far cry from 1932 when the League of Nations dispatched the Lytton Commission to secure the facts concerning Manchuria. By the time the Commission had traveled to the Pacific area, by train and by boat, and formulated its condemnation of Japan, the Japanese had taken Manchuria.

The basic resolutions placing the United Nations against aggression were passed by the Security Council in the absence of the Soviet Union. Later, when Soviet tactics made it impossible for the Security Council further to implement its resolutions authorizing resistance to aggression, the General Assembly took over the direction of events.

Although the United States contributed overwhelmingly the greatest number of military men, the burden of resistance to aggression was shared at least in some degree by a large number of United Nations members. Sixteen nations sent fighting forces. Two members sent heroic hospital units. Additional contingents could have been supplied had the logistics been arranged. Almost forty nations sent material aid of some kind. And finally, there was a United Nations command. The Security Council asked the President of the United States to name a supreme commander.

It is true that there have been other examples of collective action, when nations cooperated under a supreme commander to resist aggression. However, such resistance was never authorized by the established body of the world community. Indeed, had the League of Nations authorized resistance to aggression the day the German Army attacked Poland, the League might well have been the moral force guiding the nations resisting aggression during the Second World War. It might then have gained new stature, making unnecessary the establishment of the United Nations to take its place.

Korea gave the world hope that the nations could take collective action, if not against a great power, certainly against the satellite of a great power.

There was boldness in 1950. President Truman made a historic decision. With breath-taking speed, the United Nations responded to United States initiative. The results were felt in many directions. What might have been a chain of aggressions was interrupted and possibly a third world war averted. Western Europe particularly took heart because aggression could be met and stopped. The Atlantic Community took on additional vitality and the NATO forces developed.

It seems important to devote some attention to the way collective security operated in Korea because it gives us lessons for the future.

Certain weaknesses were revealed both in the cooperation of member states and in the machinery and procedures of collective security. The nations had not complied with Article 43 of the Charter to designate forces for use by the Security Council. Consequently, the United States, because it had military forces nearby, was called upon to make a disproportionate contribution of men and matériel.

The United Nations lacked a general staff that might have appointed a supreme commander and assessed the political consequences of his acts in the field. The Military Staff Committee provided by the Charter was unworkable. The Soviet Union was a member of it and was allied with Communist China. As an alternative, the nations with fighting forces in Korea developed an *ad hoc* basis for coordination of military efforts. Their diplomatic representatives met regularly at the Department of State. Consequently, collective action was primarily directed by Washington instead of by the United Nations. And some of the nations were altogether too willing to leave the military operations with accompanying praise and blame, to the United States. American military men were quite willing to accept this responsibility.

In retrospect, it appears that the United Nations should have been attempting negotiations for peaceful settlement while the fighting was going on.

It was a major mistake to carry the fighting north from the 38th Parallel. The United Nations resisted aggression when the Communist forces from the north crossed this line. When the original line had been reestablished and the aggressor driven across this line, the fighting should have stopped.

Moving northward toward the Yalu River gave the Chinese Government an excuse to come in. The United Nations forces suffered a tragic defeat. It would take thousands of casualties and months of effort before the military line could again be established at approximately the 38th Parallel.

Nor was the United Nations prepared for peacemaking. To everyone's consternation, there was disagreement as to who should represent the United Nations at the peace conference. The focal point of the argument was India. It was the wish of over half the members of the United Nations, but not two-thirds, that India should be at the conference. The United States opposed India's participation, partly because of Syngman Rhee's violent objection. It argued that only those nations that had fighting forces in Korea were entitled to sit at the political conference and that other members were, in effect, neutrals. This concept did not give sufficient recognition to the fact that the United Nations had collectively resisted aggression, that forty-four had voted Communist China an aggressor, and that almost forty members had supplied material aid.

Partly as a result, the nations tended to lose interest in Korea except for the sixteen that had fighting forces there. They lost the vision of this greatest effort of collective security. It may well be that the restricted point of view as to who was entitled to be represented at the peace conference gave a powerful impetus to the movement for neutralism.

Despite many difficulties, in the perspective of history, the United Nations action at the 38th Parallel may well have saved the organization from going the way of the League of Nations. Frequently the judgment of history supports the righteousness of a first instinctive action.

Retreat from Collective Security

Since the Korean fighting ended there has been a retreat from the concept of collective security. The reasons are numerous. There has been general disappointment over the failure of the United Nations to conclude the Korean affair decisively. United Nations forces are still maintaining an armistice line approximating the 38th Parallel. The Peking government and its North Korean puppet regime refuse to agree to a United Nations goal for the unification of Korea. The large and disproportionate American casualties have resulted in the Korean fighting being referred to in the United States as a war in which the United States was engaged rather than collective action under the United Nations. A shining example of collective security has been dimmed for immediate history.

The bipolarization of the world into the Western and Soviet blocs, which made the enforcement of collective security difficult in 1950, was accentuated for the next thirteen years. No combination of forces could be great enough to stop an aggressor supported by one or the other of these atomic giants. This bipolarization caused an increasing number of United Nations members to elect neutralism. Of the states admitted to the United Nations after the fighting in Korea ended, those from Asia and Africa particularly are anxious to avoid taking sides with either atomic giant.

This is not to say that the consciences of more than two-thirds of the members of the United Nations would not be touched again by another aggression, and would not respond. Nevertheless, the chances are less likely that two-thirds would declare a nation the aggressor, as they did when Peking intervened in the Korean fighting. The moral issues would have to be clearly presented if the overwhelming number of members were to be found willing to supply material aid against the aggressor, as they were in 1950.

Possible Return to Collective Security

Suddenly, in 1964, a faint beginning of a movement back to collective security as envisaged in the Charter could be discerned. It came from a source least expected—the Soviet Union. In a memorandum published July 7, 1964, the Soviet Government recognized the need of nonmilitary measures under Article 41 of the Charter, and recognized the need of resorting to Article 42 of the Charter to prevent or stop aggression, and so on. The Soviet Government contemplated that the forces called for under Article 42 would not come from permanent members of the Security Council. The Soviet memorandum reiterated the old theme that only the Security Council could direct such action.

Secretary-General U Thant referred specifically to collective security in a statement made on October 24, 1964: "Surely the only hope is to replace this military competition by growing confidence and increasing co-operation in working out an agreed system of collective security, under the principles of the Charter and within the framework of the United Nations."

Ironically, if there is to be a revival of collective security, the reason may partially be found in the breakup in the bipolarized world. With atomic war between the two giants seemingly unthinkable and with the loosening of their alliances, there has been a fragmentation of the world's power structure. Some nations might feel that they could get away with an attack on their neighbors without involving the Great Powers in nuclear war. This the Great Powers could not permit because such aggression could well lead to their confrontation. Consequently, out of the discussion of peacekeeping, etc., now going on in the corridors of the United Nations, thinking about collective security as provided for in the Charter may be revived.

In their current discussion over peacekeeping, the United States and the United Kingdom, as well as the Soviet Union, tend to turn in the direction of the Security Council. With the membership of the General Assembly large enough to be unwieldy, the Western powers may feel that collective measures should be taken if possible by the Security Council. But a much broader revival of collective security is contained in the programs for total disarmament submitted to the Geneva Disarmament Conference. These proposals will be discussed in Chapter VIII, which deals with strengthening the United Nations.

The principles of collective security are sound. The world cannot have peace without such a system. There must be universal law against aggression. Judgment must be given through proper legal procedure. There must be an obligation on the part of the nations to take action against the aggressor. The Security Council and the General Assembly have functioned in an area between Chapter VI and Chapter VII of the Charter. Some of their activities in dealing with threats to the peace go beyond the conciliatory procedures in Chapter VI. However, they stop short of the enforcement provisions of Chapter VII.

III

PEACEKEEPING, CUBA, THE SECRETARIES-GENERAL

Peacekeeping, in a broad sense, refers to the various means that the United Nations employs on the spot to prevent disputes from arising, or to stabilize the situation where trouble has arisen. It refers to mediators, truce teams, and neutral forces on guard, all to prevent hostilities while the process of peaceful settlement goes on. There have been at least nine such instances.

However, we are concerned with three formidable United Nations efforts that particularly bear the name peacekeeping. They are Suez, the Congo, and Cyprus. The backbone of a peacekeeping operation is a force of military units sent to an area to keep order while processes of peaceful settlement are under way. A United Nations peacekeeping force is different from an army engaged in collective security. It is not "mad" at anybody. It has no enemy. It is an impartial body, not there to secure a victory for one side or the other. Accompanying the military forces may be mediators and arbitrators, as in Cyprus. In the case of the Congo, a very considerable body of experts from the United Nations and its Specialized Agencies was sent to help build a stable society. So far, the military forces in these three important efforts have been contributed by the smaller states, with the exception of British forces in Cyprus. Some of the Great Powers have given logistic support. Instead of the five-power policemen contributing forces to repel aggression, as was originally contemplated, the smaller states are contributing forces to keep or restore order.

In analyzing the peacekeeping program of the United Nations in the Middle East, the Congo, and Cyprus, one will see the interplay of the Security Council, the General Assembly, and the Secretary-General.

Suez

In 1956, the United Kingdom, France, and Israel, smarting under great provocation from Egypt, decided to invade Suez. The first two vetoed a resolution in the Security Council to stabilize peace; the matter was then referred to an emergency session of the General Assembly.

Few times in the history of the United Nations have two great Western powers been subjected to more world-wide criticism than were Britain and France for this invasion. To the nations that had recently been freed from colonialism, an ultimatum and a military landing in Africa seemed like a repetition of colonial enterprises of a bygone day.

Lester B. Pearson, Canadian Minister of External Affairs, sympathized with British irritation at Egyptian provocation at Suez; yet he wished to uphold the principles of the Charter. He suggested that the United Nations send a force to Suez to make it possible for the British, French, and Israelis to withdraw. The head of the United States Delegation, Ambassador Henry Cabot Lodge, instantly supported the Canadian suggestion.

The General Assembly gave the Secretary-General seventy-two hours to recruit the UN emergency force. This he did in thirty-nine. A United Nations official made a series of telephone calls in about the following order: a call to certain Scandinavian countries, stating that the United Nations was

ready for their contingents for UNEF and that they would be
called for that afternoon; a call to the United States, asking
that the air transports the Government had promised be in
the countries designated that afternoon; a call to the Italian
Government to have a landing field ready where the United
Nations troops were to shape up; a call to the Swiss Government, requesting Swiss Air to stand by to carry the troops
from Italy to Suez; a call to the United Nations authorities
on the spot in Suez, reporting that the UN troops could be
there within forty-eight hours.

The fighting had resulted in the Suez Canal being blocked
by ships that were damaged or actually sunk. The General
Assembly instructed the Secretary-General to clear the Suez
Canal. He recruited vessels from various countries and the
Canal was cleared in advance of the target date. When
the military aspects of the Suez Canal issue were resolved the
United Nations Emergency Force moved out of Suez and
concentrated in the Gaza Strip and in the Sharm el Sheikh
area. It has remained there for nine years. The nations are
afraid to move it lest conflict break out between Israel and
her Arab neighbors.

It must be pointed out that, simultaneously with the emergency General Assembly meeting on Suez, there was an
emergency General Assembly to deal with the Soviet
invasion of Hungary. The Soviet Union had cast a veto
against a resolution in the Security Council requesting it to
withdraw its forces. This session to secure the withdrawal of
Soviet troops from Hungary was a disappointment. The Soviet Union was not responsive to public opinion, as were the
United Kingdom, France, and Israel. United Nations action
is dependent not only upon how well it can mobilize world
public opinion, but upon how well its members respond to
it. The Assembly's moral position on Hungary was clear.
With the UN membership in 1956 of seventy-seven members,

the resolution demanding Soviet withdrawal of troops was passed by a vote of 54 in favor, 8 against, and 15 abstentions.

Congo

The United Nations program in the Congo assumes the proportions of a Greek tragedy. Much that the United Nations seemed on the verge of accomplishing in 1960 now seems in danger of being lost. In the spring of 1963, it was clear that the United Nations had prevented a confrontation of Great Powers in the Congo. It had defeated the efforts of Moise Tshombe to pull Katanga Province, of which he was then President, out of the Congo. It had virtually eliminated the white mercenaries. It had laid the foundation for a constitutional government. Several thousand economic, social, and educational advisors from the United Nations and its Specialized Agencies were advising on the building of an educational system and other attributes of a modern state. The United Nations had achieved some unity of the other states of Africa so far as the Congo was concerned.

Then, at a very critical moment, the United Nations was forced to withdraw its forces. Tshombe, formerly an enemy of the United Nations, has now become Premier of the Congo Republic, and is attempting to save the state he once tried to dismember. The mercenaries are back in greater numbers. The Congo is faced with revolt. A confrontation of the Great Powers is always possible. Some Communist and Arab states are supplying war matériel in increasing amounts to the rebels. The African states seem dangerously divided.

The peacekeeping force in the Congo was ordered by the Security Council, whereas the Suez force was sent by the General Assembly. But the moments of decision were equally dramatic.

On July 14, 1960, at 3:22 A.M., the Security Council of the United Nations, in response to the frantic request of the

Congolese Government, voted to send United Nations troops to the Congo. Tired delegates responded to Dag Hammarskjöld's appeal that the peace of the world depended upon immediate action. There began a series of steps that were to involve thousands of men, loss of UN personnel, the expenditure of several hundred millions of dollars, scenes of bitterness in the General Assembly, and finally the martyrdom of Dag Hammarskjöld himself.

The Republic of the Congo had celebrated its Independence Day just two weeks previously. It was a moving ceremony, with the King of the Belgians in attendance. A few days later, enthusiasm had turned to ashes. The Congolese Army revolted. Its white officers fled. The Belgians made a general exodus from the Congo.

The Government of the Congo appealed first to President Eisenhower to send American troops. Had he done so there undoubtedly would have been a confrontation of American troops with those that would have been sent by the Soviet Union. However, President Eisenhower suggested that the Congolese Government ask help from the United Nations—indicating that when the United Nations acted, the United States would give all possible support to it.

The situation in the Congo was the most complex problem that the United Nations had yet to face. The task was literally to maintain a semblance of order and to set in motion the processes of a viable state in an area as large as the continental United States east of the Mississippi River, inhabited by fifteen million people.

The threat of Congolese disintegration and foreign intervention not only affected the Congo itself; it also threatened to affect the great part of Africa south of the Sahara.

At this point some history must be reviewed. Why did the enthusiasm of the independence ceremony turn to ashes? What was lacking in the Congo? It is not very pleasant history. In the nineteenth century, the Congo was the personal possession of King Leopold II of Belgium. The mind is staggered at the fact that one man could own that much real estate and have the power of life and death over millions of people. The natives were exploited. There were stories of atrocities and mutilations. The situation was too much even for the unenlightened colonial powers of that time. An international commission was sent there to investigate. As a result, Belgium annexed the Congo and the personal rule of Leopold gave place to control by the Belgian Parliament. The regime changed to one of paternalism.

On Independence Day, the Belgian Congo was in some ways an advanced state by African colonial standards. It had industry. Some of its people enjoyed a wage economy. There was widespread primary education through the third grade.

However, the people were not trained for self-government or for executive authority. There was not a single Congolese doctor, and only one native engineer, in a population of 15 million. There were millions of acres of land under cultivation, but no Congolese had been trained to drive a tractor. There were no native officers in the army; consequently, when the army revolted and the white officers left, there were no officers to enforce discipline.

Who could have expected that the hot winds of freedom would blow over Africa and that the colonial system would disappear overnight? Suddenly, in 1960, the Belgian Government called the native leaders of the Congo, including Moise Tshombe of Katanga Province, to a conference in Brussels. There the Government promised these leaders an independent Congo, which would include all the provinces of the Belgian Congo. The people were ill-prepared for this sudden independence.

From the decision of the Security Council on July 14, 1960, to send troops, to the time when the Congolese Parlia-

ment met at Lovanium University on August 2, 1961, the
United Nations had to deal with a situation of tragic confu-
sion. Disorders broke out in many places. There was even
rivalry between the President of the Congo, Joseph Kasavubu, and its Premier, Patrice Lumumba, as to who was
actually the head of state. The economy had ground to a halt.
People were starving. Schools had closed. The United Nations forces were rushing about the Congo like a fire department in action, putting down lawlessness here and there,
trying to establish a semblance of order, and rushing food to
starving people. Twenty thousand UN troops tried, and suc-
cessfully, to bring some order in this vast area.

The original operation in the Congo was authorized by the
Security Council. At one point, however, it was necessary to
call an emergency meeting of the General Assembly under
the Uniting for Peace Resolution to challenge what appeared
to be an effort at Soviet intervention. In the third week of
September, 1960, the Soviet Union vetoed a resolution in the
Security Council that would have asked all states to refrain
from sending military material directly to the Congo, other
than at the request of the United Nations and through the
United Nations. An emergency session of the General Assembly followed and a resolution similar to that vetoed in the
Security Council was passed overwhelmingly.

The UN operation in the Congo had another side, in addition to that of its police function. When its forces were withdrawn, on June 30, 1964, two thousand men and women
remained from the United Nations and its Specialized Agencies to continue the job of nation-building. An educational
system had to be built, doctors trained, transportation improved, finances stabilized. There is involved a very considerable operation to help an underprivileged and ill-trained
people learn to run their own affairs.

The greatest problem the United Nations peace force faced

in the Congo was that of holding the new republic together. All its leaders, including Tshombe, had agreed at the conference called by the Belgian Government, at which they were given their independence, that the Congo was to include all the provinces of the colony. The UN was faced with the danger of revolt, from the Communist sympathizers in the north to the revolt of the conservative province of Katanga in the south. Without Katanga it would have been difficult for the Congo to maintain itself as an independent state. Finally, Tshombe accepted the UN Plan of National Reconciliation.

On June 30, 1964, the United Nations forces withdrew. The dire calamities which were predicted have come true. There is general agreement that the United Nations forces were withdrawn before the Congo was ready to police itself.

There are two interrelated reasons for this withdrawal. The Congolese Government did not ask the United Nations forces to stay beyond June 30, 1964. The United Nations cannot keep forces in the territory of a sovereign state without its invitation.

The United Nations could not afford to keep its troops in the Congo longer. The Soviet bloc and France would not pay their assessments of the Congolese expenses. Many nations which could have purchased bonds or could have contributed more did not do so. Some of them were historically accustomed to spending money for unilateral action but not for collective security.

There are those who believe that the Congolese Government, granted its state of unreadiness, could have not done other than ask the United Nations troops to stay longer, had it felt they would do so in full force. But during the last six months of its occupancy the force shrank to some four thousand men. Consequently, there was a letdown in the spirit of the United Nations forces and a deterioration of their relationship with the Congolese Government.

A great mistake made was on the part of the Congolese Government in not training its own army and police force during the four years the United Nations force was there. The government had been warned that unless officers were trained their army would be little better than it was after its Belgian officers fled. This failure to train Congolese officers and policemen is attributed mainly to the vanity of the Congolese military.

In the terrible unrest following the United Nations withdrawal, President Kasavubu asked Tshombe to become Premier. Unfortunately, Tshombe is looked upon by the Africans as a tool of the colonial powers because of his long effort to bring about the secession of Katanga and his employment of white mercenaries. He had also been roundly denounced by the United States because of these activities. The African states remained fairly united in support of the United Nations action as long as UN troops were in the Congo. Many of them contributed to these forces. Now many African states are opposing Tshombe for a variety of reasons, including the ones just given. The Russians and the Chinese are carrying on their particular brand of cold war in Africa, where they are rivaling each other in how much trouble they can start.

In December, 1964, the following gains could be recorded for the United Nations intervention and peacekeeping in the Congo: (1) The United Nations saved the Congo from completely falling apart—from a collapse more serious than that which now threatens. (2) A confrontation of the Great Powers was avoided when it seemed that Russia would intervene with military forces. (3) The Congolese state was organized. Despite the present disorders and the partial breakdown, the fact remains that the United Nations set in motion the processes of statehood. (4) The United Nations undertook a vast program of economic and social building despite the withdrawal of troops. Some two thousand men and women were heroically undertaking this task.

Cyprus

The dispatch of a force to Cyprus in 1964 was another large-scale effort at peacekeeping by the UN. This force consisted of 7,000 men recruited from six countries. The island of Cyprus, freed from the United Kingdom in 1961 and admitted to the United Nations, was torn apart by its two communities, the Greek community numbering 450,000 people and the Turkish community, 50,000.

There are some interesting sidelights to the Cyprus problem. It is an example of the fact that great powers may not be able to solve a problem outside the United Nations, even though all of them are members of a regional organization. It is rather ironical that the Western powers, who constantly criticize the Soviet Union for not supporting the UN peacekeeping operations, tried to keep the Cyprus problem outside the United Nations, to be solved by the members of NATO. When this effort failed and the situation became desperate, the Security Council was asked to send a UN peacekeeping force, which it unanimously agreed to do. The British troops that remained on the island were integrated into the force. Otherwise, the troops are from the smaller states. While it was not necessary for the Secretary-General to send a team of technical assistance experts, as in the case of the Congo, he did send civilian personnel: one representative was to secure a political agreement between the Cypriote communities to stop hostilities; the other was to make an effort to find a permanent peaceful solution.

Peacekeeping Lessons

Certain lessons are evident from the United Nations peace-keeping operation. The first lesson is that the organization must be certain to have sufficient funds available to finance these important efforts. In the fall of 1964, the United Nations faced a peacekeeping deficit of over $100 million. Such a debt would not be serious to a government, but to the United Nations, without direct taxing power or assets, it is a serious matter. The problem arises because certain nations, led by the Soviet Union and France, have refused to pay their emergency assessments for peacekeeping operations. The Soviet Union insists that, since the Security Council is primarily responsible for the maintenance of international peace and security, such appropriations must be voted by the Security Council. When the Secretary-General was authorized by the General Assembly to act in the case of Suez and again by the Security Council in the case of the Congo, money was not the immediate concern. When, after the dramatic meetings of the General Assembly and Security Council, he and his aides rode to the thirty-eighth floor of the Secretariat building to telephone for troops which must be on the spot instantly to prevent catastrophe, it was not necessary to speculate where the money was coming from. The United Nations would provide it.

However, when the Secretary-General was authorized by the Security Council to send troops to Cyprus, he had to delay action two weeks while he "passed the hat" for money to send a force. In those two weeks, a Greek-Turkish war might have broken out that could have divided the NATO powers, and involved the Soviet Union and possibly the entire world.

The refusal of certain nations to pay assessments for peace-keeping operations has presented the United Nations not only with a financial but with a legal and constitutional crisis.

In 1962 the General Assembly asked the International Court of Justice for an advisory opinion, in effect, as to the binding force of emergency assessments for the cost of peacekeeping operations in the Middle East and in the Congo. The Court found that these costs are "expenses of the organization" within the meaning of the Charter. In other words, the emergency assessments were binding.

The General Assembly voted to accept the Court's opinion by an overwhelming majority.

However, the delinquents refused to be bound by these developments. The next step in the crisis was a statement of the government of the United States that it would challenge the right of certain delinquents to vote at the Nineteenth General Assembly, on the basis of Article 19 of the Charter. This Article provides that:

> A Member of the United Nations which is in arrears in the payment of its financial contributions to the Organization shall have no vote in the General Assembly if the amount of its arrears equals or exceeds the amount of the contributions due from it for the preceding two full years.

The General Assembly may make an exception in a hardship case. Article 19 also contains the following sentence:

> The General Assembly may, nevertheless, permit such a Member to vote if it is satisfied that the failure to pay is due to conditions beyond the control of the Member.

However, no one would claim that the Soviet Union and France are prevented from paying because of circumstances beyond their control.

The opening of the Nineteenth General Assembly was delayed until December 1 in the hope that the crisis might be resolved. Several ingenious proposals were made, including a plan to set up an emergency fund to which nations might contribute to help relieve the indebtedness of the organization. If the Soviet Union and others paid a sum of money into this fund to reduce their indebtedness to less than two years, their votes would not be challenged. There would be face-saving all around.

It seemed for a moment as though an agreement had been reached. However, the Soviet Union insisted on the Assembly proceeding to vote before it would indicate what it would pay. This reservation was unacceptable to the United States and other Western powers because there was no assurance that the Soviet Union would pay a sum large enough to reduce its indebtedness under the two-year figure.

Consequently, the Assembly proceeded to move to do everything it possibly could and that was necessary by consensus. The general debate continued for several weeks.

By consensus the President of the General Assembly was elected and vacancies in the Security Council and the Economic and Social Council were filled. The 1964 budget was carried over to 1965. The International Trade Conference was set up as a permanent organ of the United Nations. Certain steps were agreed to, to make possible the acceptance of funds from the Ford Foundation for the International School. It was the anticipation of the delegates that after the appointment of a committee to study the question of financing and peacekeeping the General Assembly would recess until September 1, 1965.

On the eve of recess, the representative of Albania almost succeeded in defeating these plans. At the last moment he denounced the whole procedure of recess by consensus and demanded that the Assembly proceed to organize itself and stay in session to conduct its regular business. It was assumed that he was acting on behalf of, if not at the behest of,

Communist China. The purpose apparently was to force a confrontation of the United States and the Soviet Union and to embarrass the General Assembly.

The Chair ruled that since the nations had agreed to the consensus procedure he would continue on that basis. When the Albanian delegate appealed from the ruling of the Chair, a vote could not be avoided. Ambassador Stevenson took the position that since the vote would be a procedural one and not on substance he could agree to it without violating the United States position that Article 19 must be enforced against the delinquents.

The Chair appointed a committee of thirty-three, whose task it will be to consider the question of peacekeeping and the financing of such operations. It is hoped that if a compromise can be reached for the future it will be easier to solve the problem of arrears, possibly through an emergency fund.

The dispute over the payment of peacekeeping operations has developed into a constitutional crisis, which involves the relative power of the Security Council and the General Assembly in the maintenance of international peace and security. The crisis itself will be discussed in Chapter VIII, "Strengthening the United Nations."

If the financial problem can be solved, what steps can be taken to instill a feeling of less improvisation and more permanence in the United Nations peacekeeping program? The Canadian Government was host in 1964 to a group of military experts from twenty-two countries to consider technical aspects of these special operations. Four Scandinavian countries have created stand-by forces ready for UN peacekeeping. The United Nations should know at any moment that it may call upon troops that, though trained by their respective governments, are trained under certain United Nations standards for international service. In addition, a philosophy of conduct must be formulated to guide the contingents when in the field. And the UN itself must be at all times certain as to what authority these contingents shall have. How much force may they use under varying circumstances? When shall they have the right to take the initiative to clear an area over the objection of one side? Because of improvisation, instructions in the past have at times been confusing.

The United Nations must have a permanent general staff. It must have sophisticated commanders ready for any kind of international peacekeeping operation and able to command troops of many different countries. The Secretary-General may not always been able to find a person of the caliber of Major General E. L. M. Burns, of Canada, for instant command of peacekeeping troops.

The need for UN forces in the Middle East, in the Congo, in Cyprus, is an indication of the complex and serious problems that will call for peacekeeping forces in the future. The United Nations has had very considerable experience, some considerable success and some obvious disappointments in these larger efforts as well as in less-known peace-keeping operations. A tradition, a technique, a method has grown as a result of these experiences. It should be codified.

The Role of the Secretary-General

The Secretary-General is the third factor in the UN's machinery for the peaceful settlement of disputes. The expanding role of this office has been one of the most important developments in the history of the organization. It has resulted from courage and wisdom on the part of three successive Secretaries-General, and because of the existence of certain vacuums which the General Assembly and the Security Council have asked the Secretary-General to fill.

The authority of the Secretary-General stems from Chapter XV of the Charter. The Secretary-General "shall act in that capacity in all meetings of the General Assembly, of the Security Council, of the Economic and Social Council, and of the Trusteeship Council, and shall perform such other functions as are entrusted to him by these organs." And Article 99 states that he may "bring to the attention of the Security Council any matter which in his opinion may threaten the maintenance of international peace and security." Articles 100 and 101 provide for the independence of the Secretary-General and his staff in the performance of their duties.

The first sentence of Article 97 provides that "the Secretariat shall comprise a Secretary-General and such staff as the Organization may require." Trygve Lie made the first liberal use of this article. At one time, prompted by necessity and using bold improvisation, he recruited a force of some seven hundred guards, radio technicians, chauffeurs, automobile mechanics, and others to accompany United Nations missions in the field. Someday this group may be called the beginning of a United Nations peace force.

At the emergency meeting of the Security Council in 1950, Trygve Lie, using his authority under Article 99 of the Charter, called the attention of the nations to a breach of peace at the 38th Parallel in Korea.

Early in 1950, Trygve Lie formulated ten principles of peace to be accomplished in twenty years. One of them suggested that the question of Chinese representation in the United Nations be dealt with decisively, a step which in retrospect many people, including Americans, wish had been taken then. Trygve Lie journeyed from New York to Washington to London to Paris to Moscow to present his ten principles to the major governments.

Under Dag Hammarskjöld and now U Thant, the role of the Secretary-General has been further expanded.

Time and again, Mr. Hammarskjöld dared to visit various capitals to seek a reduction of tensions or a settlement of disputes. He traveled widely to encourage nations in the fulfillment of their United Nations obligations and to find out how the United Nations could help. In the winter of 1959-60, Mr. Hammarskjöld concluded an extensive visit to Africa. There he undertook to find out what were the most effective steps the United Nations should take to fulfill its objectives of a dynamic international society on behalf of nations still struggling for freedom or of those who had just attained it.

Mr. Hammarskjöld was frequently asked by United Nations bodies to undertake missions and to make settlements on the spot that could not be spelled out by the General Assembly. He was asked to visit Communist China to secure the release of United Nations prisoners of war. He was asked by the General Assembly to recruit a United Nations force at the time of the Suez crisis and to recruit vessels to clear the Suez Canal. He was authorized to establish a United Nations presence in the Middle East.

In the former Belgian Congo, Mr. Hammarskjöld was given the overwhelming task of recruiting a United Nations peace force to arrest chaos there and of sending experts from many walks of life to help build a viable state.

Much of the development of the role of the Secretary-General was due to the genius of Dag Hammarskjöld, assisted by an exceptionally able staff. In early 1960, however, he himself warned that there was a limit to what the nations could expect of his office, that the powers could not dodge their responsibilities of meeting certain problems in the Security Council or the General Assembly.

Tragically, the Fifteenth General Assembly witnessed an attack by the Soviet Union upon the office of the Secretary-General and on Dag Hammarskjöld personally. The move was calculated to destroy the bold initiative that he had undertaken so vigorously in the Congo. The U.S.S.R. proposed its troika plan: to substitute for a single Secretary-General a presidium of three—one representing the socialist bloc of states, another the "neutrals," and a third the "Western military bloc."

Mr. Hammarskjöld's reaction to the challenge that he resign was to reply that he would stay as long as the smaller states, which need the United Nations so badly, wished him to stay. His courage and buoyancy remained undaunted until his death. He had the support of the vast majority of the members.

The small states overwhelmingly rejected the troika plan as fallacious. To them the Secretary-General has played a particularly sympathetic role. Statesmen from new countries have sought his advice and guidance, something representatives from the older, established powers do not need to do. The small states were quick to see that a three-headed Secretary-General would rob them of this independent friend. Such a plan would mean extending the veto now enjoyed in the Security Council to the Secretariat. The members of the United Nations recognized in 1961 that whereas there might be a well-defined and disciplined Communist bloc voting as a unit, there were no solid "neutral" or "Western military" blocs as such. And by 1964 the well-disciplined Communist bloc was breaking up.

So anxious were the members of the United Nations for the maintenance of an independent Secretary-General that U Thant was unanimously elected Acting Secretary-General after Hammarskjöld's sudden death, and then Secretary-General for a full term without compromising his office and without accepting "troika."

It is hard to compare the three Secretaries-General. Trygve Lie met his greatest crisis over Korea. Dag Hammarskjöld faced his greatest crisis over the Congo. U Thant's courage was demonstrated in 1962 when he boldly interposed his office, backed by the Security Council, between the United States and the Soviet Union—two great nuclear giants—on a collision course over Cuba.

U Thant has recruited and directed the United Nations peacekeeping forces in Cyprus. He has sent teams of investigators and established United Nations presences in several troubled situations.

In one respect U Thant has had a harder role because the United Nations has been faced with virtual bankruptcy because of the failure of some states to pay their peacekeeping assessments. Consequently, he has been held back in peacekeeping initiatives because of the debilitating effect of critical United Nations finances.

As the twentieth year of the United Nations opens, U Thant is confronted with two serious crises. One is the increasing military conflict in Southeast Asia. He has offered his good offices. Eventually the United Nations must be involved in the settlement of this crisis in a very important way.

The constitutional crisis, which developed out of the problems of peacekeeping and UN financing, may be solved and the whole concept of peacekeeping and collective security advanced. This may be the most constructive development to take place during U Thant's Secretary-Generalship.

Cuba

The Cuban crisis in 1962 demonstrated that the United Nations had both the authority and the skill to interpose itself between two superpowers who were on a collision course.

While the United Nations has found the United States and the Soviet Union on opposite sides of the fence on many issues before it, this is the first time there was an absolute, clear-cut issue, in which they were the sole protagonists. It was the general view that another precedent had been established, another milestone achieved, in the growing strength of the United Nations to meet ever greater tests.

The week of October 22, 1962, seemed one of the most dangerous to peace since the Second World War. For the first time, leaders of the two countries actually contemplated what a nuclear attack would be like. A great part of the world feared nuclear destruction.

Several statesmen share the credit for pulling the world back from disaster. On October 22, 1962, President John F. Kennedy informed the American people in an address televised from the White House that Soviet missiles were being placed on launching pads in Cuba. The President announced simultaneous actions—a naval blockade and a request for an immediate meeting of the United Nations Security Council.

The President refused to be swept into a U.S. invasion of Cuba or a bombing of the bases, as some people urged him to do. And, as he pointed out, Chairman Khrushchev had made a "statesmanlike decision" when he agreed to discontinue shipments of offensive missiles and to order those already in Cuba dismantled.

We are concerned particularly with the role of the United Nations in this Cuban crisis. Let us picture the United States and the Soviet Union deadlocked in the Caribbean without a Security Council where they could appear, and where the hopes of all mankind could be expressed. It is hard to see how one or the other could have pulled back from such a perilous position. Indeed, one could say that if there had been no United Nations the two giants might have confronted each other with disaster. It has been said many times that the United Nations has made the difference between the uneasy peace in which the world now lives and catastrophe.

At the Security Council there were scenes of great drama.

At last the confrontation of the two powers was real. Each one had enough nuclear weapons to destroy all life on this planet. No other member of the United Nations—not even the best-armed, and certainly not the unprepared new states—could stand against them. Nevertheless, representatives of many countries spoke in the Security Council or in the corridors of the United Nations. They were physically unarmed, but they were morally and legally armed. They were armed with the hopes of mankind and with the principles and the law of the Charter. Their spokesman was U Thant, who at a strategic moment made a proposal in the Security Council, which was accepted.

On October 24, 1962, Acting Secretary-General U Thant informed the Council that at the request of a large number of delegations he had sent identically worded appeals to President Kennedy and to Chairman Khrushchev, asking them to suspend voluntarily the arms shipments and quarantine measures for a period of two to three weeks, and to enter into immediate negotiations for a peaceful solution. He also appealed to Prime Minister Castro to assist in finding a way out of the impasse by halting work on the installations under discussion. U Thant declared himself available to all parties for whatever services he might be able to perform.

During the dramatic Security Council debate, the Secretary-General received favorable replies from President Kennedy and Chairman Khrushchev.

On the following January 7, a joint letter from the Soviet Union and the United States to the Secretary-General expressed the appreciation of the two governments for the Secretary-General's efforts. It went on to say that while not all the related problems in the situation had been resolved, the two governments believed that "in view of the degree of understanding reached between them on the settlement of the crisis and the extent of progress in the implementation of this understanding, it is not necessary for this item to occupy further the attention of the Security Council at this time."

Although it is frequently said that the United Nations does not have the means to coerce the Great Powers, it is a fact that a surprising number of the major problems before it have directly or indirectly dealt with those nations. The first act of the Security Council was to persuade the Soviet Government to pull its troops out of Iran. UN resistance to aggression at the 38th Parallel in Korea was at first indirectly against Communist China and the Soviet Union and later against China directly. In the Suez crisis, the United Nations necessarily had to persuade the British and the French to withdraw from Suez. The program of the United Nations in the Congo was partly to prevent a confrontation of the Great Powers. The Western powers, members of NATO, and the Soviet Union were very much concerned with the problem of Cyprus. The action in the Cuban crisis concerned the United States and the Soviet Union directly. Whenever the Great Powers wanted to avoid a confrontation, the United Nations provided the means by which this confrontation could be avoided.

Frustrations and Neglect

Against the successes of the United Nations in meeting disputes must be balanced the frustrations, the delays, the neglects, and the failures.

The causes of some of the conflicts with which the United Nations deals go back to antiquity. These causes cannot be uprooted in one single series of meetings. This is one of the reasons that, in some instances, the United Nations has been able to stop fighting and secure an armistice, but has not been able to translate the armistice into peaceful and permament settlements. The members will agree to action that the United Nations recommends in order to stop fighting that might produce a world catastrophe. Too frequently they are not willing to make the additional sacrifice of their immediate national interests for a permanent peace settlement. The illustrations are numerous:

The United Nations at great cost of life and money finally stopped aggression at the 38th Parallel in Korea. It secured an armistice. It has not been able to move from an armistice to a peace settlement that would unify that unhappy peninsula.

The United Nations stopped the fighting between India and Pakistan when thirty thousand troops were mobilized for instant war. Its truce teams are still guarding the truce lines in Kashmir. However, the United Nations has not been able to conduct the plebiscite because of India's refusal, although both parties had agreed to it.

The United Nations secured armistice agreements between Israel and the Arab states. Mixed commissions supervise the armistice lines and the United Nations Emergency Force protects one of them. But the UN has not been able to translate the armistice agreements into final peace settlements. In violation of the Charter, the Arab states claim to be in a state of war with Israel.

The vast majority of the statesmen from the smaller powers wish to avoid choosing sides in the cold war. A few, however, find it advantageous to play up to one great power or another and use such protection to threaten aggression. President Sukarno, of Indonesia, furnishes an example of this kind of conduct. He objected to the federation of Malaya and other territories into the larger state of Malaysia. Finally, he agreed that if the Secretary-General would send a team of observers to see if the wishes of the inhabitants of these territories had been properly consulted he would withdraw his objection. The United Nations observers so found; whereupon Sukarno repudiated his word and threatened to crush

Malaysia. He feels he can get away with it because he has the moral and physical support of the Soviet Union and Communist China.

That he was right in this conclusion was proved by the Soviet veto of a mild resolution in October, 1964, calling on both Indonesia and Malaysia to refrain from the threat or use of force and to respect each other's territorial integrity and political independence. Sukarno has been encouraged to further aggressive demands on his neighbors because his insistence on annexing West Irian—formerly Netherlands New Guinea—paid off. The United Nations administered the area until sovereignty could be transferred from The Netherlands to Indonesia "provisionally." The word provisionally is in quotes because although the agreement provides that in ten years the illiterate inhabitants of West Irian may vote as to their future, Sukarno makes no bones of the fact that he expects to keep the territory.

Much of the unrest, bitterness, and even warfare that President Nasser has been able to stir up in the Middle East is because of his capacity to challenge the Great Powers to bid against each other in the cold war.

The powers have at times ignored their obligations to present to the UN, when other means have failed, disputes whose continuance threatens the peace of the world.

The problem of Indochina and its three successor states should have come before the United Nations years ago. In 1953 the Government of the United States, along with other governments, wanted the entire problem brought to the United Nations, in the same way that the problems of the Dutch possessions were brought to the UN when continued tensions threatened international peace and security. France was making an effort to regain her former province of Indochina, which she had lost during the war. Consequently, she objected to the matter being brought to the United Nations;

she insisted it was a domestic matter. The powers did not bring pressure to bear on France, a permanent member of the Security Council, as they did on The Netherlands. The French lost Indochina. Three separate states were created. Despite several general meetings held outside of the United Nations at Geneva, to neutralize the states, the fighting grows more serious, particularly in Vietnam. Thousands of American troops are engaged.

Despite all American efforts to strengthen the Republic of Vietnam, the authority of the state is gradually being whittled away because of instability from within and aggression from without. Looming over the whole area is the ominous shadow of mainland China, now an atomic power.

It would seem that the time has arrived—indeed, it arrived years ago—for the Government of the United States to ask the United Nations, presumably the General Assembly, to help find a peaceful solution so that war may be averted and American troops withdrawn with the integrity of South Vietnam, Cambodia, and Laos preserved. One cannot tell exactly what form a United Nations debate and subsequent action might take. But since neutralization and military intervention have failed, Charter obligations and logic suggest turning to the United Nations in the hope it can bring the parties together to arrest the accelerating drift toward general war.

Even if no UN solution can now be found, such presentation could strengthen the American position. The Secretary General has offered his good offices.

On April 7, 1965, President Johnson said the United States was prepared for "unconditional discussions" on peace in Vietnam. The President asked U Thant to initiate as soon as possible a vast plan for cooperation in economic and social development in Southeast Asia in which North Vietnam could share, and in which industrial states such as the U.S.S.R. could participate.

IV

DISARMAMENT

For the first time in the tedious history of disarmament negotiations the nations have accepted general and complete disarmament under effective international control as the final goal. They unanimously accepted this goal in a resolution of the Fourteenth General Assembly on November 20, 1959. Until then, the nations had talked about controlled, regulated, and limited armaments. Never before had they accepted total disarmament with all the implications for a strengthened United Nations.

The first breakthrough in disarmament after this historic act of the General Assembly was the limited nuclear-test-ban agreement signed in Moscow August 5, 1963. The United States, the United Kingdom and the Soviet Union, with the Secretary-General of the United Nations in attendance, agreed to abstain from testing nuclear devices on land, on the sea or in the air. The agreement was signed shortly thereafter by over one hundred members of the United Nations.

Turning again to the Fourteenth General Assembly, the address of Chairman Nikita Khrushchev crystallized the objective of a world without armies, without navies, without air forces, without military training schools, without weapons of any kind.

The head of the United States Delegation to the United

Nations, Ambassador Henry Cabot Lodge, made an historic contribution to the discussion. He said that if there were general disarmament there would need to be "institutions to preserve international peace and security and to promote the rule of law." He proposed the study of three questions:

1. What type of international police force should be established to preserve international peace and security?
2. What principles of international law should govern the use of such a force?
3. What internal security forces, in precise terms, would be required by the nations of the world if existing armaments were abolished?

One by one, various nations in the Fourteenth Assembly caught the spirit. Many of them urged immediate steps that should be taken to facilitate total disarmament. Many warned of the length of the road before the final goal was attained. However, all of them accepted the final objective, which was sponsored and passed unanimously by the General Assembly.

Since then, proposals to achieve the final objective in precise steps have been proposed by the United States, the United Kingdom, and the Soviet Union.

Sixty-five Years of History

The movement for disarmament can be said to have lasted, so far, for sixty-five years—that is, if one believes that it began with the initiative of Czar Nicholas II of Russia. During these sixty-five years, there have been two world wars and a fantastic increase in armaments. The Czar, worried about the rising tide of armaments, suggested that a peace conference be held at The Hague in 1899. Military men, particularly from the German Empire, succeeded in blocking any effective steps toward the reduction of arms. An international court was proposed at the conference, but not set up because the nations could not agree on how the judges were to be selected. The most that could be agreed upon was the establishment of The Hague Court, consisting of a panel of judges from which nations seeking arbitration could draw arbitrators. Neither did the Second Hague Conference meeting in 1907 make any progress toward disarmament. Forces were already massing for the First World War.

More practically, then, one might say that the disarmament movement began with the League of Nations. This was the first effort to make disarmament and collective security part of the processes of organized community life.

From the beginning of the League of Nations there has been a debate as to which comes first, collective security or disarmament. The classic point of view has been that nations will not give up armaments until they find in collective security the orderly processes of the international community. Individuals on a frontier are only persuaded to give up their guns if the community has the means of producing law, with a sheriff to enforce it and a justice of peace to administer it.

So it is with nations. It is argued that nations will not give up their arms until they can find greater security in an international system of law and order. However, armaments may in themselves add to a sense of insecurity. In an address to the Sixteenth General Assembly of the United Nations, the late President John F. Kennedy said:

> Men no longer debate whether armaments are a symptom or a cause of tension. The mere existence of modern weapons—ten million times more powerful than any that the world has ever seen, and only minutes away from any target on earth—is a source of horror and discord and distrust. Men no longer maintain that disarmament must await the settlement of all disputes—for disarmament must be a part of any permanent settlement.

Covenant and Charter Compared

Since the modern movement for disarmament began with the League of Nations, it is worth comparing the League of Nations Covenant and the United Nations Charter on the subject. The Covenant was more precise on disarmament and the Charter is more precise on collective security. The United Nations Charter contains surprisingly little on disarmament compared with the League of Nations Covenant. The disarmament obligations of the latter were more positive and binding. Article 1 (2) of the Covenant made willingness to accept arms regulations a price of membership. In addition to giving guarantees of its sincere intention to observe its international obligations, an applicant "shall accept such regulations as may be prescribed by the League in regard to its military, naval and air forces and armaments."

The Covenant recognized the influence of armaments on peace when it stated in Article 8 (2) the Council shall "formulate plans for such reduction for the consideration and action of the several Governments." The Covenant further provided that such plans would be subject to reconsideration and revision at least every ten years. Article 9 provided for a permanent commission "to advise the Council on the execution of the provisions of Articles 1 and 8 and on military, naval and air questions generally."

On the other hand, the United Nations Charter neither designates disarmament as one of the overriding tasks of the organization, nor does it make willingness to agree to disarmament regulations a price of membership. The word disarmament first appears in the Charter under Chapter IV, Article 11. This article states that the General Assembly "may consider the general principles of cooperation in the maintenance of international peace and security, including the principles governing disarmament and the regulation of armaments, and may make recommendations . . . to the Members or to the Security Council or to both."

Under Article 26 of the Charter the Security Council shall be responsible for formulating, with the assistance of the Military Staff Committee, plans to be submitted to the members for the establishment of a system for the regulation of arms. Article 47 provides for the establishment of this Military Staff Committee, which shall advise and assist the Security Council "on all questions relating to the Security Council's military requirements for the maintenance of international peace and security, the employment and command of forces placed at its disposal, the regulation of armaments, and possible disarmament." Apparently the regulation of armaments was considered feasible—disarmament possible.

What is the reason for the difference in emphasis? The First World War, the first to be waged with what then seemed the weapons of modern science, had shocked mankind. The Central Powers were disarmed, the Austro-Hungarian Empire fragmentized. The Soviet Union was not then considered a formidable military power. Disarmament agreement among the heavily armed states—the United States, the United Kingdom, France, and Japan—seemed attainable. Indeed, in retrospect, disarmament appears so much easier then than now that one wonders why the League did not succeed in achieving it. If an arms agreement had been reached could German rearmament have been blocked, thus avoiding the tragic history of the postwar years, with the final catastrophe of the Second World War?

The League of Nations disarmament efforts failed because of the futility of striving for technical agreements while ignoring the necessity of political agreements that would furnish a guarantee against aggression. For American supporters the later days of the decline of the League of Nations were tragic indeed. As James T. Shotwell has said, the United

States pushed disarmament by mathematical ratio while ignoring at all times the need for collective security. Renunciation by Germany of the arms agreement of the Treaty of Versailles and her subsequent withdrawal from the League of Nations were steps leading to the final collapse of peace.

One should not discount the seriousness of the disarmament steps of the League of Nations. The organization proceeded very far. The late General George V. Strong, Chief Military Adviser to the United States Delegation during the greater part of the League of Nations Disarmament Conference, testified to this fact. He stated, shortly after the atomic bombs were dropped on Japan, that the technical phase of the League's work, essential to the preparation of any disarmament convention, was of permanent value and, in fact, so far completed that not more than three months would be required to bring it up to date. General Strong died when the atomic bomb was quite new. His statement was made as scientists and military men were crossing the threshold of thermonuclear weapons.

The framers of the United Nations Charter reacted to the experiences of the League. They placed collective security first. A series of collective security articles reached their climax under Article 43, by which the members agreed to make available to the Security Council armed forces and assistance for action against an aggressor.

It would be a mistake to give the impression that disarmament was not in the minds of the framers of the Charter. However, the fate of the world for the next years seemed to them to be in the hands of the five big "policemen" with permanent seats in the Security Council. If they remained united, they could keep the peace of the world during the reconstruction period. They could agree among themselves on a reduction of armaments, both for themselves and for other nations. The building of the organization, therefore, and the establishment of a system of collective security seemed to be the first concern of the founders. Consequently, while the first disarmament obligation of the League of Nations Covenant is to be found in Article 1, that of the Charter is to be found in Article 11, and then in less positive terms.

However, between the time that the Charter was completed at San Francisco and the organization set up, the security provisions of the Charter were thrown out of balance: The United States ushered in the atomic age. Secretary of State Dulles, referring to this situation, said in part: "As one who was at San Francisco in the spring of 1945, I can say with confidence that had the delegates at San Francisco known we were entering the age of atomic warfare, they would have seen to it that the Charter dealt more positively with the problems thus raised." Disarmament might well have been one of these problems.

During the two decades since the Charter was drafted, the arms race has moved at a fantastic pace. Two startling phrases illustrate it: One, "nuclear deterrent," is the phrase used to describe the necessity of the United States and the U.S.S.R., the atomic giants, remaining at peace with each other, because in attack and instant retaliation both would be destroyed. The other phrase, "operation overkill," describes the situation in which these two nuclear giants continue to go on building beyond that which would be necessary to destroy each other many times over.

The late President Kennedy, in a press conference on August 20, 1963, said that the United States had enough nuclear weapons to kill three hundred million people within the first fifteen minutes of the outbreak of war. Thus, at the time of the signing of the limited nuclear-test-ban agreement on August 5, 1963, there were enough nuclear weapons to destroy life on earth.

The United Kingdom has belonged to the nuclear club for

some time without making any effort to rival the stockpiles of the two giants. France, for prestige purposes, has entered the club more aggressively than the United Kingdom. Communist China entered on October 16, 1964, by exploding a nuclear device—one more sophisticated than had been predicted. Japan, Sweden, and Israel, among other states, can enter the club whenever they are willing to stand the necessary expense. However, possession of a nuclear device does not automatically produce the bombers or other means of delivery to an enemy target.

The First-Phase Negotiations

The first phase of United Nations disarmament negotiations lasted from the establishment of the Atomic Energy Commission down to the moment when the Soviet Union announced it had exploded an atomic device. The very first resolution of the First General Assembly Meeting in London was the appointment of an Atomic Energy Commission, at the suggestion of the United States, the United Kingdom, France, and the Soviet Union.

Shortly thereafter, the United Nations established its headquarters in New York City. A dramatic scene was presented when the Atomic Energy Commission, composed of the members of the Security Council plus Canada, sat around the horseshoe table in the temporary Security Council room at Hunter College. Bernard Baruch was speaking. He presented the plan of the United States for the regulation and control of atomic weapons. It was an amazing plan indeed. Mr. Baruch proposed that an International Atomic Development Authority have a monopoly on the world's production of atomic energy. The Authority would have exclusive control of all atomic activities, from the mining of raw material to the production and use of fissionable fuel. In addition to owning and managing all uranium and thorium mines, refineries, chemical separation plants, and reactors, it was to have the exclusive right to engage in atomic research. It could also punish the individual or the nation for violation of the atomic energy agreements without a Great-Power veto interfering. At this historic moment, the United States made the most far-reaching and dramatic proposals for supranational authority that any government has ever presented anywhere. It amounted to world government in a very important field of human activity.

The Soviet representative rejected the entire plan as "thoroughly vicious and unacceptable." The Soviet Union then adopted the line that it has consistently followed ever since: Outlaw atomic weapons with a bare minimum of international control. Undoubtedly, a major, basic Soviet objection to the Baruch plan, although not presented in so many words, was that under it the United States would forever be the only power knowing the secrets of nuclear weapons. The United States might scrap all its nuclear weapons, all peaceful atomic plants might be operated by the United Nations, but in the Russian mind the United States would always have the advantage of having the experience of making the Bomb. Russia's growing pride demanded that it, too, make bombs before permitting them to be renounced.

The Soviet Union also feared that the proposed International Atomic Development Authority would be dominated by Western nations.

The Second Phase

The second phase of disarmament negotiations began when the United States ceased to have a monopoly of atomic bombs. It was announced at the Fourth General Assembly that the Soviet Union had exploded a nuclear bomb. Nuclear rivalry was then accelerated. In 1952, the United States announced that it had achieved the hydrogen bomb. The Soviet

Union followed. The race continued through the development of guided and intercontinental missles. The rivalry between the two powers continued in outer space. The Soviet Union announced that it had launched its first Sputnik into the orbit of the earth. The United States followed with its Explorer. The Soviet Union placed a satellite into the orbit of the moon and photographed the opposite side of that body. The United States launched a satellite into the orbit of the sun. The possibility was opened up that nuclear devices might be carried into the heavens.

In discussing all disarmament proposals, the Soviet Union has consistently opposed any lessening of the veto power that it holds in the Security Council. The United States and other nations have been trying to break out of the restrictions of the veto in matters of inspection and control. Along with fear of the abolition of the veto is the Soviet fear of international inspection. In Russia a built-in suspicion of having other people see what is going on antedates the Communist regime. The fear of observation from outside goes back to Czarist days. For a great number of years the Soviet Union has repeated the propaganda slogan "Abolish the Bomb" without yielding substantially to the principle of inspection. At times, the Russians have suggested self-inspection.

Space does not permit a review of the number of General Assembly resolutions passed or the number of United Nations commissions and committees meeting in New York, London, and Geneva that have dealt with the problem of disarmament. The Atomic Energy Commission was the first disarmament body established by the United Nations. It was followed in 1947 by the establishment of the Commission for Conventional Armaments. In 1952, a new Disarmament Commission with the same membership—the members of the Security Council plus Canada—took over the functions of the two. In 1954, a subcommittee of this commission was appointed, consisting of the four permanent members of the Security Council—the United States, the U.S.S.R., the United Kingdom, and France—plus Canada.

One would not want to give the impression that in the many meetings of the Disarmament Commission of twelve and its subcommittee of five nothing was done. A vast number of proposals came from all of its members. At times, they seemed on the verge of a breakthrough. But the cold war became colder. Technical developments moved so fast that proposals for disarmament could not keep up with them.

In 1958, the twelve-nation Disarmament Commission of the United Nations was abandoned for a Disarmament Commission to be composed of representatives of all the members of the United Nations.

Two events in 1960 and 1961 seemed to take the nations far back from the spirit that produced the resolution for total disarmament in 1959. The first was the catastrophic breakup of the summit conference between President Eisenhower and Chairman Khrushchev before it had a chance to get under way. It followed the U-2 incident. In 1961 the Soviet Union broke the moratorium on nuclear testing that had been in effect for several years. The United States followed with a series of tests.

Again the mood changed. Two significant events ocurred in the Sixteenth General Assembly: The U.S.–U.S.S.R. Joint Statement on disarmament and the agreement to set up the eighteen-nation disarmament committee. In response to Assembly resolutions urging renewed disarmament talks, the United States and the U.S.S.R., represented by John J. Mc-Cloy and Valerian Zorin, respectively, negotiated a "Joint Statement of Principles" to guide the disarmament discussions, which was then submitted to the General Assembly. It was in this Assembly that the late President Kennedy said:

Today every inhabitant of this planet must contemplate the day when this planet may no longer be habitable. Every man, woman, and child lives under a nuclear sword of Damocles, hanging by the slenderest of threads, capable of being cut at any moment by accident or miscalculation or by madness. The weapons of war must be abolished before they abolish us.

The U.S.–U.S.S.R. Joint Statement of Agreed Principles provided that disarmament would be general and complete, and war would no longer be an instrument for settling international problems. Such disarmament would be accompanied by reliable procedures for peaceful settlement of disputes and arrangements for maintaining peace in accordance with the Charter. States would have only such non-nuclear arms as are agreed to be necessary for internal order and personal security of citizens. States would, further, provide agreed manpower for a United Nations peace force. Succeeding paragraphs spelled out steps for achieving the final objectives.

Subsequently, in the Assembly's Political Committee, the United States and the Soviet Union, negotiating under the terms of a resolution submitted by India, agreed on the formation of an eighteen-nation Disarmament Committee, which would convene in Geneva in March, 1962, to discuss the test-ban and general disarmament questions. However, the refusal of the French Government to send a representative reduced participation in the Committee to seventeen nations.

The eighteen-nation committee and some that preceded it are not technically United Nations committees. The inspiration, however, for their formation and subsequent conferences came from United Nations resolutions. The conferences use the United Nations buildings and facilities at Geneva; they submit reports to the General Assembly; their plans contemplate considerable expansion of United Nations machinery.

One measure that received serious consideration in the discussion in the eighteen-nation Disarmament Committee in the summer of 1962 was the issue of the cessation of war propaganda. Although the United States and the U.S.S.R. agreed on a joint declaration banning war propaganda, the U.S.S.R. at the last moment repudiated it. Other partial measures under consideration included methods of preventing accidental war.

In the meantime, the great importance that the United States attaches to total disarmament and the concern it has for the danger of the arms race, was demonstrated by the establishment by Congressional authority of the United States Arms Control and Disarmament Agency in 1961—the first such independent agency established by any government. Governments have had their departments of national defense, which were concerned with maintaining armaments. No government before had ever established a department to be concerned with disarmament. The Agency is autonomous. Its director is responsible both to the Secretary of State and the President.

The first paragraph of Section 2 of the Congressional Act establishing the Agency, entitled "Purpose," states: "An ultimate goal of the United States is a world which is free from the scourge of war and the dangers and burdens of armaments; in which the use of force has been subordinated to the rule of law; and in which international adjustments to a changing world are achieved peacefully. It is the purpose of this Act to provide impetus toward this goal by creating a new agency of peace to deal with the problem of reduction and control of armaments looking toward ultimate world disarmament."

The eighteen-nation Disarmament Committee, minus France, has had before it three documents: the United States Program for General and Complete Disarmament, presented on September 25, 1961; the United States Outline of Basic Provisions of a Treaty on General and Complete Disarmament in a Peaceful World, proposed on April 18, 1962; and the Draft Treaty on General and Complete Disarmament submitted by the Soviet Union on March 15, 1962. The Conference also has before it resolutions of the United Nations General Assembly.

Programs for general disarmament were discussed in the plenary sessions of the Committee of Eighteen, where the two nuclear giants submitted the most comprehensive plans in the history of the negotiations. The United States plans were noteworthy for their proposals for strengthening the peace-keeping machinery of the United Nations: They would use every available means for the peaceful settlement of disputes; a United Nations Peace Observation Corps would be organized on a permanent basis; and a United Nations Police Force, progressively equipped with agreed types of armaments necessary to enforce the peace, would be established. In addition, the parties to the treaty would undertake to accept the compulsory jurisdiction of the International Court of Justice.

Significantly, the Soviet plan also provides for strengthening the United Nations as the principal institution for the maintenance of peace, and for national forces to be made available in the Security Council.

While for many years the chief dispute over opposing plans for general disarmament has centered on the Soviet reluctance to agree to adequate inspection, the emphasis has now shifted to the differences on timing and extent of various disarmament measures, or phasing, as it is called. Some similarities between the two plans are evidence that the years of United Nations debates have not been fruitless. Both three-stage plans provide for the establishment of an International Disarmament Organization within the framework of the United Nations, with powers to ensure the implementation of disarmament measures through means of verification; for the reduction of conventional armaments to the level necessary for the maintenance of internal order; for the elimination of nuclear weapons and delivery vehicles; for the withdrawal of foreign troops and the dismantling of bases; and for the prohibition of weapons of mass destruction in orbit (outer space).

The General Assembly asked a group of economists from ten different countries to present a report on the impact of disarmament on world economic conditions. A unanimous report was submitted in March, 1962. Its principal conclusion was that, with proper planning, a major reduction in the burden of armaments would *not* produce a depression, as is frequently contended, but would lead instead to world-wide improvement of living conditions.

After months of hope, frustration, and disappointment, the United States, the United Kingdom, and the Soviet Union finally signed the limited nuclear-test-ban agreement in Moscow on August 5, 1963. The agreement has been signed by almost all the members of the United Nations. It was acclaimed for several reasons: First, it could possibly be an indication that the three powers have turned toward cooperation. The agreement might be the beginning of a series of steps to reduce political tensions. Second, it could be the first step on the long road to the goal of total disarmament. Third, it meant a virtual end to the poisoning of the atmosphere by fallout from the tremendous nuclear explosions conducted by the Soviet Union and the United States.

Three major questions were left open in the optimism of the summer of 1963—and they are still open:

To what degree will the parties remain committed to make the agreement work and to proceed with the next steps?

How serious is it to the world that France and Communist China have not signed the agreement?

Can the nations, on this partial success, build and make

additional progress toward general and complete disarmament?

Following the partial test-ban treaty, there has been the resolution of the General Assembly to bar nuclear weapons from outer space, the unilateral reductions of the military budgets of the United States and the Soviet Union, and the mutual cutbacks in production of fissionable material for military purposes by these two countries and the United Kingdom.

U Thant, in reporting to the Nineteenth General Assembly, said: "More significant progress in achieving some measures of disarmament has taken place since the summer of 1963 than in all the years since the founding of the United Nations."

An outline of specific steps that could be undertaken shortly was given in the 1965 New Year's message of President Lyndon B. Johnson to the leaders of the Soviet Union. The President said:

> Arms control remains especially urgent; nothing can contribute more to the hopes of mankind for the future. During the months ahead I hope we can work for practical agreements to this end. We can and should move to limit the spread of nuclear weapons; to achieve a verified worldwide comprehensive test ban; to make a cutoff of fissionable material production for weapons coupled with measures to safeguard the peaceful uses of nuclear power; and to agree on a verified freeze in existing offensive and defensive strategic nuclear delivery systems.

V

HUMAN RIGHTS AND
FUNDAMENTAL FREEDOMS

The United Nations is concerned with human rights for the individual and freedom for the nation.

A plaque on the wall of a conference room in the Fairmont Hotel in San Francisco declares:

25 April–26 June 1945

> In this room met the Consultants of forty-two national organizations assigned to the United States Delegation at the Conference on International Organization in which the United Nations Charter was drafted. Their contribution is particularly reflected in the Charter provisions for human rights and United Nations consultation with private organizations.

It marks a historic meeting. Crowded into this room on May 2, 1945, were the members of the United States Delegation, headed by Edward R. Stettinius, Jr., and the consultants. The latter presented a letter signed by many of them, asking that the Charter contain additional and stronger phrases pledging the nations to respect human rights and fundamental freedoms. The author of this book was very anxious that the Charter provide for a commission on human rights. He was afraid that otherwise postwar reactions might prevent creating such a commission. Dramatic speeches were made by the consultants. Mr. Stettinius in his report to the President noted that it was the intervention of the consultants that resulted in the provision for the Commission on Human Rights.

Obviously, the delegates from other countries, supported by their people at home, likewise wished the Charter to be strong in its provision for guaranteeing human rights and fundamental freedoms. They had seen the origins of the war grow out of the violation of these freedoms in Germany and Italy.

Freedom from fear was among the peace objectives stated in the Atlantic Charter. This declaration, signed by Prime Minister Winston Churchill and President Franklin D. Roosevelt in 1941, contains a remarkable phrase of nineteen words, only one of which has more than one syllable. It could be recommended to English classes as a classic of Anglo-Saxon prose. It reads: ". . . that all the men in all the lands may live out their lives in freedom from fear and want."

Four years later, the second paragraph of the Preamble of the United Nations Charter pledged the nations "to reaffirm faith in fundamental human rights, in the dignity and worth of the human person, in the equal rights of men and women and of nations large and small. . . ." And the third purpose stated under Chapter I contains the following phrase: "and in promoting and encouraging respect for human rights and for fundamental freedoms for all without distinction as to race, sex, language, or religion. . . ."

No part of the Charter better illustrates the obligations that the members undertake for both individual and collective action than the human rights provisions. Article 55 gives the United Nations, as an organization, obligations to promote human rights. Article 56 declares: "All Members pledge themselves to take joint and separate action in co-operation with the Organization for the achievement of the purposes set forth in Article 55." The nations stopped short, however, of taking an obligation to give the United Nations itself authority to enforce human rights and fundamental freedoms.

The Economic and Social Council is charged by the Charter with the over-all task of implementing the human rights obligations. This body may prepare draft conventions in this field for submission to the General Assembly. It may call international conferences. And lastly, Article 68 provides that it "shall set up commissions in economic and social fields and for the promotion of human rights. . . ."

The protective arm of the human rights provisions of the Charter is extended to the peoples of the world who do not enjoy self-government. Under Chapter XI, members of the United Nations who have assumed responsibility for the administration of non-self-governing peoples accept as a sacred trust the obligation to assist these peoples in the progressive development of their political institutions. And under Chapter XII, establishing the international trusteeship system, one of the obligations of the trust powers is "to encourage respect for human rights and for fundamental freedoms for all without distinction as to race, sex, language, or religion. . . ." Inhabitants in the trust areas have the right to petition the Trusteeship Council for redress of grievances.

The International Labor Organization, which antedates the United Nations by several decades, marks one of the first substantial references to human rights on an international level. Similar obligations concerning human rights are reflected in the constitutions of other Specialized Agencies.

The operating heart of the United Nations machinery for the promotion of human rights is the Commission on Human Rights. Mrs. Franklin Delano Roosevelt was its first Chairman. It was decided early that the Commission should produce an international bill of human rights. The bill was to be divided into three parts. The first was to be a declaration of human rights, containing fundamental principles to which all peoples could aspire. The second was to be a covenant stating in treaty form those obligations of the declaration that could be so stated, ratified, and become part of international law. The third part of the bill was to contain machinery for enforcement.

The Universal Declaration of Human Rights

The first of the three parts has been achieved. It was near midnight on December 10, 1948, when the General Assembly, meeting in Paris, adopted the Universal Declaration of Human Rights. The delegates had before them the draft, which represented two years of discussion and deliberation in meetings of the Commission. The Declaration was adopted by 48 votes in favor, none against, and 8 abstentions. Before its adoption, Mrs. Roosevelt stated that it was first and foremost a declaration of the basic principles to serve as a common standard for all nations. It might well become the Magna Carta for all mankind.

The wording of the Declaration lacks the moving drama of the American Declaration of Independence or the French Declaration of the Rights of Man, because the United Nations document had to be translatable into five different languages. Granting this handicap, it reads amazingly well.

When the Declaration was adopted, the President of the General Assembly said: "It is the first occasion on which the organized community of nations has made a declaration of human rights and fundamental freedoms, and it has the authority of the body of opinion of the United Nations as a whole, and millions of men, women and children all over the world many miles from Paris and New York will turn for help, guidance and inspiration to this document."

The record will show that his prediction was correct. Indeed, the Declaration marks one of the most remarkable developments in the law of nations. Although not to be considered binding as a treaty, it has developed such authority that it not only is a source of law but is coming to have the force of law. In his Dag Hammarskjöld Memorial Lecture on December 4, 1963, Jacob Blaustein said: "Nevertheless, in the fifteen years since its adoption, it has acquired a political and moral authority which is unequalled by any other international instrument with the exception of the Charter itself. It is no exaggeration to say that no international instrument has ever received the same acceptance on all levels of society."

Pope John XXIII, referring to the Universal Declaration of Human Rights in his encyclical *Pacem in Terris,* said:

> There is no doubt, however, that the Document represents an important step on the path towards the juridical-political organization of the world Community. For in it, in most solemn form, the dignity of a person is acknowledged to all human beings; and as a consequence there is proclaimed, as a fundamental right, the right of free movement in the search for truth and in the attainment of moral good and of justice, and also the right to a dignified life. . . .

In a memorandum from the Office of Legal Affairs of the United Nations in 1962 it was stated that, while a resolution cannot be made binding upon member states in the sense that a treaty is binding upon them, "However, in view of the greater solemnity and significance of a 'declaration,' it may be considered to impart, on the part of the organ adopting it, a strong expectation that Members of the international community will abide by it. Consequently, in so far as the expectation is gradually justified by State practice, a declaration may by custom become recognized as laying down rules binding upon States."

Various resolutions of the General Assembly have been based upon principles of the Declaration. Many of its articles have been incorporated into peace treaties, trust agreements, and the constitutions of new states. It has been cited as an authority by domestic courts. The member states are expected to use its principles as a standard of measurement in their reports each three years as to the condition of their domestic human rights.

The European Convention for the Protection of Human Rights is based on the Universal Declaration of Human Rights. This document was signed on the fourth of November, 1950, by the foreign ministers of thirteen European states. The Convention represents a significant contribution to the cause of human rights by the Council of Europe. Its Preamble refers to the Declaration of Human Rights "proclaimed by the General Assembly of the United Nations on the tenth of December, 1948. . . ." The Convention then states: "Being resolved, as the Governments of European countries which are likeminded and have a common heritage of political traditions, ideals, freedom and the rule of law, to take the first steps for the collective enforcement of certain of the rights stated in the Universal Declaration. . . ."

The influence of the Declaration goes on. Its principles tend to become part of the common law of nations.

Two powerful declarations in the history of the United Nations are, first, the Universal Declaration of Human Rights, adopted in 1948, and, second, the Declaration on the Granting of Independence to Colonial Countries and Peoples, adopted in 1960. Indeed, these documents are closely related because the latter is based on the principle of self-determination, which is one of the principles of the Universal Declaration. The next chapter in this book, on the freeing of colonial areas, has a very close relationship to this chapter on human rights.

Covenants on Human Rights

With the adoption of the Declaration statesmen anticipated that work would start on the second part of the international bill of human rights, the Covenant on Human Rights. Indeed, John Foster Dulles, one of the United States delegates to this historic Assembly, so predicted. More than fifteen years have passed since the Dulles prediction. The nations have not yet completed the second and third parts of the bill. The statement of human rights in treaty form has shown itself to be a more formidable task than anticipated. There early developed a difference of opinion between the older democracies and the new states. The former thought of a covenant on human rights in terms of the basic civil rights which are part of the Western system of justice. The newer states wished to place equal or even greater stress on economic rights. Many of their statesmen spoke from a background of hunger and misery. They insisted that the right to eat and the right of a man to support his family are basic human rights.

While the Western powers were sympathetic to the latter point of view, they doubted that it could be expressed in an international treaty. The economic conditions of many states vary greatly—from poverty to prosperity, from a primitive economy to industrialization. Under such conditions, it is difficult to draft a treaty guaranteeing the right to a job or to social security.

A compromise was reached. It was decided to draft two covenants, one on civil and political rights and one on economic, social, and cultural rights. The two covenants were passed on to the General Assembly, hopefully for adoption in the year 1954. At each General Assembly, the Third Committee has continued to debate and accept additional clauses to the two covenants.

The Secretary-General said that it is not surprising that the drafting of the two covenants has taken so long. Between them, he said, they "cover almost the whole of the relations between the individual and society, something which, as recently as a generation ago, was considered as coming within the exclusive domestic jurisdiction of states."

On November 14, 1961, Salvador P. Lopez, of the Philippines, Chairman of the Assembly's Third Committee, stressed the importance of the forthcoming Assembly debate on the draft covenants: "This Committee has been engaged in a revolutionary effort to lay down a suitable philosophical and juridical groundwork for the new world order, and its members may well be regarded as the Encyclopedists of the atomic age."

The Third Committee of the General Assembly has almost completed the general provisions and substantive articles of both covenants. However, proposals for articles relating to the rights of the child and the right of asylum have not yet been adopted.

The task of writing two covenants has shown itself to be so formidable that there are those who believe it may be necessary in the long run to draft a whole series of covenants. Each would deal with a specific human right, which could be put into treaty form and ratified.

Implementation

The third part of the International Bill of Human Rights was to be machinery for enforcement. Implementation is the term generally used to define the clauses looking to some measure of enforcement that would be added to each of the two covenants. In each case a different approach is made to the problem of implementation. As far as the Covenant on Economic, Social, and Cultural Rights is concerned, ratifying nations will be asked only to report to the United Nations on the progress that they make toward the achievement of these rights. Presumably, these reports would be reviewed sympathetically by the Economic and Social Council, with a view to assisting the nations, if necessary, toward achievement of the standards laid down in the Covenant.

However, in the matter of civil and political rights, the measures of implementation may be more forceful and precise. According to the plan as it now exists, there would be established a fact-finding and conciliation organ known as the Human Rights Committee, to which States Parties could complain that other States Parties had violated their obligations under the Covenant. The Human Rights Committee would then attempt to bring about a settlement. Failing this, the Committee would publish a report indicating whether in its opinion there had been a violation of the Covenant. There would also be a right of recourse to the International Court of Justice.

Specific Human Rights Covenants

There have been a number of human rights conventions produced by the United Nations itself or by its Specialized Agencies. It may be worth referring to several of them here.

The Genocide Convention was unanimously adopted by the General Assembly on December 9, 1948. It was then submitted to the members for ratification. The word genocide was coined to describe what the Germans attempted to do—to destroy a whole people on the basis of race, culture, and religion. Over sixty-five governments have deposited instruments of ratification or accession.

In 1950, the General Assembly adopted the Convention on the Political Rights of Women. This Convention was the product of the Commission on the Status of Women. It entitles women to "vote in all elections on equal terms with men, without any discrimination" and "to hold public office

and to exercise all public functions, established by national
law, on equal terms. . . ."

In 1955, the United Nations, through the Economic and
Social Council, proceeded to draft a new antislavery convention. It found some so-called "refined" forms of slavery that
had not been covered by the original League of Nations anti-
slavery convention. The Convention was adopted in 1956.

Another important convention, "Concerning the Abolition of Forced Labor," was adopted by the International
Labor Organization in 1957. This Convention binds ratifying states not to use any form of forced labor "as a means of
political coercion or education or as a punishment for holding or expressing political views or views ideologically opposed to the established political, social or economic system;
as a method of mobilising and using labour for purposes of
economic development; as a means of labour discipline; as a
punishment for having participated in strikes; as a means
of racial, social, national or religious discrimination."

In 1953, the Government of the United States took a dis-
astrous step backward that seriously compromised its leadership in the field of human rights, as well as weakening the
human rights movement itself. This was the year in which
"Brickerism" reached its crest. A strange, unreasoning sentiment was whipped up against international human rights
covenants. As a compromise to this sentiment, and in the
hope that it would defeat a movement to amend the United
States Constitution to limit Senate ratification of human
rights conventions, the United States Secretary of State, John
Foster Dulles, announced that the Administration would not
submit any human rights agreements to the Senate for ratification. He further said that the Administration would not
press for ratification of agreements that had been submitted
to the Senate. Thus the United States served notice that no
matter how ably drafted the forthcoming human rights

covenants might be, it would not make any effort to ratify them. This declaration weakened the hand of the United States representative on the UN's Human Rights Commission and in the General Assembly to influence these documents favorably. It also served notice that the United States would not press for ratification of the Genocide Convention, which had already been submitted to the Senate.

Fortunately, President John F. Kennedy reversed the negative policy on July 22, 1963, when he asked the Senate to ratify the United Nations conventions on slavery, forced labor, and the political rights of women. The Genocide Convention was not mentioned.

Some of the conventions are so in harmony with American ideals or constitutional practice that it is hard to see what objections could be made to their ratification. The United States was one of the leaders in denouncing the Nazi crimes that led to the Genocide Convention. Secretary of State Dean Rusk, in describing the forced labor convention to the Senate, said that the subject matter comes within the scope of the Thirteenth Amendment to the United States Constitution which provides that "Neither slavery nor involuntary servitude, except as a punishment for crime whereof the party shall have been duly convicted, shall exist within the United States, or any place subject to their jurisdiction."

During the period when it was cool to the ratification of human rights conventions, the United States Government compensated somewhat, apparently in the only way it could, by moving in the Commission on Human Rights and the Economic and Social Council for a different type of program for the promotion of human rights and fundamental freedoms. In this, it has been successful.

The U.S. Action Program

In 1953, the American representative on the Human Rights Commission submitted the United States Action Program. This program consisted of three parts: the first, a program of periodic reports on human rights; the second, a series of studies on human rights; the third, technical assistance in certain human rights fields.

The first part of the program provided that governments of states which are members of the United Nations and Specialized Agencies are asked to submit reports to the Human Rights Commission every three years. These reports describe developments and progress achieved and the measures taken to safeguard human liberty in metropolitan areas and in non-self-governing and trust areas. Again, the influence of the Declaration of Human Rights is shown. The reports are to be based on the principles enumerated in the Declaration. The reports shall also be based on the rights of all peoples to self-determination. The new states have insisted that human rights agreements recognize this right.

The Commission on Human Rights does not sit in judgment on a particular nation. Rather it studies the reports in order to give the Economic and Social Council a picture of human rights conditions throughout the world and to submit recommendations for their improvement.

The second part of the U.S. Action Program comprises a series of studies on specific rights. Considerable progress has been achieved. The program provides for a series of studies on discrimination: in education, religious rights and practices, occupation and employment, political rights, emigration and travel. They are to be carried on under the auspices of the Human Rights Sub-Commission on Prevention of Discrimination and Protection of Minorities. In each case so far, the studies have resulted in proposals for a standard of conduct by government and individuals to be incorporated in the form of recommendations or conventions, or both. When the subject of the study falls within the area of a UN Specialized Agency, that body is asked to participate in the drafting of the required document. For illustration: the International Labor Organization produced a convention on discrimination in employment. The problem of discrimination in education was turned over to UNESCO. That body adopted a recommendation and convention at its General Conference in November of 1960. The Sub-Commission is now working on religious rights and political rights. It will be seen that in the new program the United States Government has not been able to avoid international conventions completely.

The third part of the U.S. Action Program consists of advisory services in the field of human rights. This is in the nature of a technical assistance program and follows a resolution of the General Assembly of 1955, which provides for three types of assistance: (1) provision of experts; (2) provision of fellowships and scholarships; (3) organization of seminars.

It is twenty years since the human rights provisions were incorporated in the Charter of the United Nations adopted at San Francisco. It is seventeen years since the adoption of the Universal Declaration of Human Rights.

The Human Rights Score

What is the score on human rights observance throughout the world? The moral insight and determination by which people proclaim a charter of freedom is not maintained in the day-by-day process of carrying the principles of the Declaration into daily life.

Certainly the Charter of the United Nations goes very far in defining human rights and fundamental freedoms as an obligation for the men and nations in the United Nations to advance. Certainly it goes far in setting up machinery for carrying out these obligations. The Declaration of Human Rights probably has had as wide acceptance throughout the world as any document in history outside the Charter of the United Nations itself. Some specific covenants have been drafted and widely ratified. The nations of Western Europe have set up an international system for the enforcement of human rights, including a court.

Large areas of the world remain, however, where the principles of the Declaration may have been adopted but are not understood or carried out. There is still a considerable area of the world where a knock on the door at midnight may mean the concentration camp for fancied political crimes or evil thoughts. There remains a large area where basic civil rights such as freedom from arbitrary arrest or freedom of speech are almost unknown.

Old-fashioned chattel slavery is prevalent in some of the Arab countries of the Middle East. The British Anti-Slavery Society has estimated that seven hundred thousand men and women are held as slaves. So fearful are the nations of offending the Middle East countries, because of their strategic importance, their oil interests, and the Suez Canal, that few voices indeed have been raised to protest this slavery in United Nations meetings.

And it comes as a shock to the American people to realize that their own denial of human rights to the Negro, accompanied by riots and bombs, puts this country on the defensive in a great part of the world.

So far as South Africa is concerned, apartheid is an official policy rather than a custom for which the government apologizes.

If the work of the United Nations might be divided into the prevention of war, economic and social cooperation, and the advancement of human rights—how does progress in the last area compare with the first two? The machinery that the United Nations and its Specialized Agencies have created and developed is much more elaborate for the prevention of war and the achievement of economic and social cooperation than for the advancement of human rights.

The reasons are understandable. In the critical political situation in which the world has lived since the end of the First World War, the prevention of war and the settlement of disputes seems to have demanded paramount attention. And critical attention seems necessary for over half the human race that is aware of its misery and its helplessness. It should also be pointed out that while the prevention of war deals in the main with the external conduct of people, and the work of economic and social cooperation contains benefits for mankind, the enforcement of human rights deals more than the others with individual practices. Any effort to enforce human rights in a specific nation appears to be interference in that nation's domestic practices. This explains why as enlightened a country as the United States will go far in advancing the first two objectives but has not yet ratified a single human rights covenant.

The Charter of the United Nations provides for the enforcement of peace. It falls short in providing for the enforcement of human rights. Most of the members have agreed that since they take an obligation under the Charter to advance human rights and fundamental freedoms they may discuss violations and even appoint committees of investigation. This they did in the case of apartheid in South Africa. However, there is a considerable difference between debate and enforcement.

It is also generally agreed that the nations would have a right to proceed under Chapters VI and VII of the Charter if the continuance of a violation of human rights was so serious as to threaten the peace of the world. This has been the basis of the African demand for sanctions against apartheid. However, such UN enforcement of human rights has never been undertaken.

Several procedures are being advanced to strengthen human rights enforcement. It is now proposed that the nations provide annual instead of triennial reports on human rights observance. The Human Rights Commission would specify what particular subjects should be reported on in each year. It is further proposed that the reports be submitted to the nongovernmental organizations with consultative status so that they may present their views. Thus a considerable public opinion would be developed as a means of moral enforcement.

The Charter provision that some nongovernmental organizations be given consultative status originated with James T. Shotwell, who was one of the consultants at the San Francisco Conference. Professor Shotwell and several colleagues from the nongovernmental organizations agreed that there should be a breakdown between private citizen groups and official bodies. As a result, it was provided in Article 71: "The Economic and Social Council may make suitable arrangements for consultation with non-governmental organizations which are concerned with matters within its competence. Such arrangements may be made with international organizations and, where appropriate, with national organizations after consultation with the Member of the United Nations concerned."

Jacob Blaustein, in his Dag Hammarskjöld Memorial Lecture, proposed that as a step forward "the General Assembly or the Secretary-General might appoint an independent personality who would be a kind of international commissioner dealing with human rights, bearing perhaps the title of United Nations High Commissioner for Human Rights." His thought was that such a High Commissioner could "lend his good offices to governments and be available at their request to investigate situations where there have been alleged violations of human rights; he could assist underdeveloped countries in the organization of various institutions for the promotion of human rights" and "he could assist the Commission on Human Rights in its review of the periodic reports from governments . . . ."

If the nations advance toward permanent peace, it is inevitable that human rights will be advanced and safeguarded. In an address to the Fiftieth Anniversary Dinner of the American Jewish Committee, Dag Hammarskjöld said, "We know that the question of peace and the question of human rights are closely related. Without recognition of human rights we shall never have peace, and it is only within the framework of peace that human rights can be fully developed."

VI

THE HOT WINDS OF FREEDOM

Over seven hundred million people have thrown off the yoke of colonialism in the last twenty years. This marks one of the greatest periods of social revolution in history. It is comparable to the scientific revolution, which unlocked the forces of atomic energy and opened the horizons of outer space.

Throughout several centuries, the European powers had extended their colonial sway over a large part of the world. In the main it meant control of territories far removed from the mother country, and usually the dominance of white people over colored.

The Second World War set in motion forces for the rapid liquidation of the colonial system. The war, its suffering, its artificial prosperity, its friendly or unfriendly invasion of soldiers, touched every part of the world. The colonial system could not slumber after the experience of the Second World War. Twice in a generation the Western world had lost caste by wars it inflicted on the world. Some of the colonial powers promised a greater degree of self-government to their dependent peoples if they would fight for the mother country.

The delegates to the San Francisco Conference anticipated this awakening. They wrote into the Charter obligations to advance self-determination, self-government and even independence, which they undoubtedly would not have agreed to in some of their more reactionary moods following the war. However, it is doubtful whether anyone in San Francisco anticipated how fast the liquidation of the colonial system would come about or that the world would be fragmentized into so many small political units.

The procedures for the orderly liquidation of the colonial system are to be found in the Charter itself—specifically, Chapters XI, XII, and XIII. Under Chapter XI, headed "Declaration Regarding Non-Self-Governing Territories," the members assumed wide obligations for the administration of territories whose people had not yet reached a full measure of self-government. Under this Chapter, each ruling power is "to transmit regularly to the Secretary-General for information purposes, subject to such limitation as security and constitutional considerations may require, statistical and other information of a technical nature relating to economic, social, and educational conditions in the territories for which they are respectively responsible other than those territories to which Chapters XII and XIII apply." Later in this chapter it will be clear how far beyond these procedures the United Nations has gone.

Chapters XII and XIII establish the International Trusteeship System and the Trusteeship Council. It will presently be seen how the trusteeship system has been partially liquidated.

The United Nations early played an important part in the granting of independence to colonial areas. The first legislative act of the General Assembly was to exercise authority conferred upon it by the treaty of peace with Italy, in which it was to dispose of the Italian colonies if the Great Powers should fail to agree over such disposal. The Great Powers did disagree; the General Assembly set the terms for eventual independence of Libya, Eritrea, and Somaliland. The United

Nations actively administered Libya for a time until a viable state could be established.

When the British decided to surrender their Palestine mandate, the British Government asked the General Assembly to fill the vacuum by assuming authority to determine the future of the area. After reviewing the report of its subcommittee, the Assembly agreed to the partition of Palestine and the establishment of the State of Israel.

The United Nations had much to do with the arrangements for the independence or self-government of some colonial areas, such as the Dutch possessions now consolidated in an independent Indonesia. The Security Council insisted on dealing with the problem because it was a situation the continuation of which was a threat to international security.

The process has been cumulative. Nations having won their independence agitated in the General Assembly, and outside it, for the independence of others.

Some colonial areas achieved their independence through a growing liberal policy on the part of the colonial powers themselves. The United States gave the Philippines its independence. The British recognized the right of the subcontinent of India to partition and of the two parts to become independent. India and Pakistan elected to remain members of the British Commonwealth.

One of the most amazing tributes to the British people occurred in the General Assembly in 1957, at the time the Federation of Malaya was admitted to membership. One by one, members of the British Commonwealth rose to pay tribute to the United Kingdom for granting independence to another part of its empire—and which had elected to become a member of the Commonwealth. Other members of the United Nations joined in the tribute, the majority speaking in English. One was aware in this inspiring moment that the tight little island of Great Britain, with its principles of justice and freedom, had spread its influence throughout the world. More than one-tenth of the members of the United Nations are former parts of the British Empire that won their independence after the United Nations was established. Two-thirds of this number elected to remain members of the British Commonwealth.

France was slower to accept the inevitability of independence for parts of the French empire. However, in one stroke, General de Gaulle granted independence or membership in the French Community to the major portions of the empire, except for Algeria. The opening day of the Fifteenth General Assembly presented a most dramatic scene. Eleven times the President of the General Assembly announced that a certain state in Africa had been recommended to the General Assembly by the Security Council for membership in the United Nations. Eleven times he asked the Chief of Protocol to escort the new delegation to their seats. In that one morning occurred the liquidation of the French Empire and the birth of the French Community. All these states were sponsored by France for membership.

Many observers believe that one of the most important, if not the most important, contribution the United Nations has made to world peace has been in helping some colonial territories to freedom and in receiving most of the new states into the family of nations. Had the revolt of almost one-third of the world's population taken place in a world of anarchy, the violence, dislocation, and ideological conflicts would have been a serious threat to world peace. Secretary-General U Thant has said:

> In ... the trusteeship field, or to put it more correctly, in the field in which the United Nations has been engaged to accelerate the emergence of the dependent countries into independent ones, the United Nations record has been most impressive. The United Nations

has been the sole agency which has been responsible for the creation of many independent states, particularly in Asia and Africa. . . . This, in my view, is the most impressive and most remarkable achievement of the United Nations in the past seventeen years.

Approximately 2 per cent of the world's population is still deprived of self-government or independence. However, this number constitutes the hard core of the problem. Portugal, in her control of Angola and Mozambique, and South Africa in control of the large territory of Southwest Africa, refuse to accept the inevitability of self-determination for dependent peoples.

The trust areas were, first of all, to be the old League of Nations mandates. It will be remembered that the League of Nations mandates system was the first world recognition of responsibility for dependent areas and their preparation for self-government.

The United Nations Trusteeship System would include, in addition to the old League of Nations mandates, territories that might be detached from states as the result of the Second World War and territories voluntarily placed under the trusteeship system. The Union of South Africa, now the Republic of South Africa, was the only mandatory power that did not transfer its mandate to United Nations trusteeship. The General Assembly sought an advisory opinion of the International Court of Justice as to the legality of this refusal. The Court advised that the Union of South Africa must continue to administer the territory under the terms of its League of Nations mandate. In other words, its obligation to the world community for the administration of this area could not be escaped. Repeated General Assembly resolutions have condemned the evident intention of the Republic of South Africa to annex Southwest Africa.

The first body of the United Nations to become obsolete

may well be the Trusteeship Council. This body, according
to the Charter, is to be composed of a representative from
each member administering a trust territory, the permanent
members of the Security Council, and representatives from
as many other members elected to the Trusteeship Council
as may be necessary to ensure an equal balance between
administering and nonadministering powers. As many areas
have been freed, the Council has been proportionately reduced in size. In fact, its entire existence may be unnecessary
within a few years unless given new tasks in the decoloniza-
tion field.

Ironically, the only trust areas that may remain in the fore-
seeable future could be the United States trusteeship for the
old Japanese-mandated islands and the Australian trusteeship
for New Guinea. The former embraces some eighty thousand
indigenous people scattered over islands that dot an area of
the Pacific as great as that of the continental United States.
And yet, if all of these islands were put together they would
not make a land mass larger than the state of Rhode Island.
Obviously, these scattered eighty thousand people cannot
compose a viable state. They could, however, become self-
governing in partnership with the United States and so no
longer come under the trusteeship system.

A comparison of the attitude toward non-self-governing
peoples of the Third General Assembly in 1948 and that of
the Fifteenth General Assembly in 1960 is most revealing.
The Third General Assembly took what was considered an
advanced step when it established a committee to assess the
reports that the powers were obligated to submit to the
Secretary-General on economic, social, and educational conditions in the territories for which they were individually
responsible. The colonial powers objected to the appointment of such a committee because it was not provided for in
the Charter. However, the Assembly argued logically that if

reports were to be submitted to the Secretary-General, some committee should assess them. Why not a committee of the General Assembly?

The Fifteenth General Assembly, in 1960, adopted a Declaration on the Granting of Independence to Colonial Countries and Peoples. It passed with 90 votes in favor and 9 abstentions. This resolution will forever be hailed as the charter of independence for dependent peoples. Its effect will be as far-reaching as that of the Declaration of Human Rights, of which it is a companion.

The heart of the resolution is contained in Articles 1, 2, and 3.

Article 1 provides that subjection of peoples to alien subjugation, domination, and exploitation constitutes a denial of fundamental human rights, is contrary to the Charter of the United Nations and is an impediment to the promotion of world peace and cooperation.

Article 2 states: All peoples have the right to self-determination; by virtue of that right they freely determine their political status and freely pursue their economic, social and cultural development.

Article 3 states that: Inadequacy of political, economic, social or educational preparedness should never serve as a pretext for delaying independence.

The Sixteenth General Assembly reaffirmed the Declaration of the Fifteenth General Assembly. This time the United States voted for the Declaration instead of abstaining. The Seventeenth General Assembly expanded to twenty-four members a special committee whose purpose it is "to examine the application of the Declaration, to make suggestions and recommendations on the progress and the extent of the implementation of the Declaration." A report was made by this Committee to the Eighteenth General Assembly concerning each of the areas of the world where peoples still live in "subjugation" to the rule of others. The Eighteenth General Assembly dissolved the Committee on Information from Non-Self-Governing Territories and requested the Special Committee of Twenty-Four to take over its functions.

In addition to a few fairly large areas, most of the remaining are small islands and island groups and what have been called "bits and pieces" of population. The Secretary-General estimates there are some sixty dependent territories that come under the purview of the declaration on decolonialism. It is hardly possible that these small areas could become viable states capable of maintaining an independent economy, conducting foreign relations, or fulfilling the obligations of United Nations membership. Some of them will undoubtedly maintain economic and cultural relations with a larger power on a basis of choice. It is not anticipated that the Virgin Islands, for example, would ask for other than free association with the United States.

Not all freed people may want to join the United Nations. Western Samoa is an example of an area of small population approved for membership in the United Nations, but which wisely decided that it did not wish immediately to assume the responsibilities of membership. It maintains economic ties with New Zealand.

The general supervision of the welfare of these small fragments of peoples may be a new role for a reorganized Trusteeship Council.

With the sudden entrance of so many very small states, particularly from Africa, many questions are asked about their effect on the United Nations. The problem of so many new states in the General Assembly is giving rise to much concern as to the capacity of that body to make sober judgments. For illustration, the Assembly's Committee of Twenty-Four to examine the status of decolonialism similarly is bent upon concerning itself with the affairs of peoples who are quite content with the self-government they now enjoy. Inasmuch as Puerto Rico has chosen to be part of the American commonwealth in place of independence or statehood freely offered to it, it seems an effrontery for the United Nations committee to concern itself with this arrangement.

Suddenly, at the Nineteenth General Assembly and at meetings of the Security Council in December, 1964, a number of African states exhibited a feeling of racism that was shocking to those who had worked for independence of African colonial areas. The humanitarian airlift to save hundreds of non-Africans caught in Stanleyville and surrounding communities was portrayed as colonialism and imperialism.

In the eyes of some observers, the wide disparity of size and resources of these new members creates political and economic imbalance. For illustration, thirty-five states from the continent of Africa representing almost one-third of the votes in the General Assembly have a total of less than 9 per cent of the world's population.

Indeed, the rapid fragmentation of the colonial world into small political units, some of them hardly viable as states, leads to the speculation that eventually the Assembly must come to some kind of weighted voting. This will be discussed in Chapter VIII, "Strengthening the United Nations." Indeed, some have gone so far as to challenge the juridical concept of the "sovereign equality of states" as a basic order of future international society.

The less pessimistic agree that the new states will present the United Nations with challenges for some time to come. The more mature members of the United Nations must regard the situation not with panic, but with sympathy, understanding, and perspective.

What are the benefits to the United Nations of the entrance of the new states? What problems do they present to the United Nations? What are the gains to the new states? The major gain to the United Nations is that despite all the difficulties of so many additional political units the United Nations is approaching universality. If it is to be the legally constituted organization of the society of nations, it must be universal; it cannot be a club of like-minded people. All sovereign states must be bound by its law. The United Nations must be a reflection of the world as it is, and through this reality gain strength to absorb the most dissonant elements, and, without destroying variety and differences, unite all in the consensus of community life. Possibly one fatal drawback of the League of Nations was the fact that not more than two-thirds of mankind could be represented in the organization by governments of their own choosing.

Membership in the United Nations is the first desire of many of the new states. Some of them applied for admission only a few hours after the last orator had finished speaking at their independence ceremonies. Most of them wanted membership in the United Nations first and recognition by individual powers second. For this there are several reasons: their delegates can speak in the General Assembly as vigorously and as long as can the representatives of the Great Powers; their membership in the United Nations holds out the hope of freedom from absorption by any power and freedom from having to choose sides in the cold war power struggle.

The United Nations bodies serve as a training center not only in diplomacy but also in democracy and parliamentary practice. The statesmen of the older countries must be patient as some of the new statesmen learn these practices. An observer must not be condescending in making these remarks; many of the new statesmen are highly sophisticated and were trained at Oxford, the Sorbonne, or Harvard—others have much to learn. Indeed, the United Nations has now established a training institute where aspiring statesmen from the new countries may be trained in the ways of administration and diplomacy.

A new type of diplomatic center is developing adjacent to

the United Nations. Many of the newer and smaller states cannot afford to establish embassies in over a hundred capitals. Consequently, their statesmen maintain contacts with the entire world through their missions to the United Nations, where they can be in touch with representatives of over a hundred other countries.

Obviously, new states vary greatly in background, capacity, and size. Some of them, such as India, have a heritage of hundreds of years of civilization, from which they will make a particularly important contribution to the fabric of international society. Other states are emerging from a tribal system, which, despite a sometimes complex form of organization, has less to contribute to modern society. The more sophisticated ones have a richness of experience, philosophy, and viewpoint to add to the mosaic of international society. These people feel their world is more devoted to peace and less materialistic than the Western world. Sometimes, to the Western world, their profession of neutrality seems perplexing. But to these states the West seems preoccupied with a scientific race that has a military objective.

There are those who wish that freedom might have come to the colonial world, particularly the African part of it, more gradually and in a more orderly manner. Certainly, one might have wished that more energy had been devoted to the preparation of peoples for self-government. Freedom, however, does not necessarily come in a logical way. When a sentiment for freedom sweeps an area, it cannot be held back. Freedom cannot be rationed. People are going to have it whether they are ready for it or not, peaceably or explosively. And who shall deny this right? In the twentieth century these people have the same right to declare themselves free and make their own mistakes as had the thirteen American Colonies or the republics of Latin America.

The older members of the United Nations, in meeting the problems presented by the new states, particularly those from

Africa, must consider the human as well as the juridical side of the problem. It takes patience, tolerance, and understanding to do so.

Many of the new states have roots of nationalism that go back for many centuries. Others have known only tribal loyalty; nationalism came after independence. Indeed, one of the great problems of some of the African states is that the colonial powers as they divided the continent according to their own needs were not particularly concerned with tribal loyalties. Consequently, in some cases the present boundaries cut across strong tribal lines.

In assessing the bitterness that was apparent in some of the things that various African statesmen said in the Security Council in December, 1964, one must think of two words: *slavery* and *color*. One must read again the sad and grisly tale of King Leopold's policies in the Belgian Congo. One must reread the monstrous stories of the slave traders to understand some of the bitterness of black Africa, of which ambitious leaders and Communist agitators could take full advantage. It is hard for Africans to respond to the friendship of the United States, which this country would offer so gladly, because there are emblazoned across the newspapers they read the savagery of Mississippi, the bombing of black children in a church in Birmingham. It will take many years, and great patience and understanding, to alleviate this problem.

The trend toward smaller political units is in full swing. Following the admission of eleven French-speaking African states to the United Nations on September 20, 1960, the French Ambassador said to Andrew Cordier, then Executive Assistant to the Secretary-General, "You must be very happy today because France has brought in eleven new members." Cordier replied, "I would be happier if you had brought in five."

Unfortunately, such federations as the Central African

Federation broke up and the contemplated Caribbean Federation did not jell. And yet it is hard to see how common sense, prompted by economic necessity, can avoid the creation of federations. A very hopeful development in Southeast Asia is the joining of Malaya, Singapore, Sarawak, and North Borneo into the Federated State of Malaysia. Tunis, Morocco, and Algeria have for some time called themselves the Malgreb States and constantly emphasize their intention of federating. Zanzibar and Tanganyika have joined to form Tanzania. Egypt and Syria have an on again, off again federation called the United Arab Republic. Great possibilities seem inherent in the Organization of African Unity, cooperating with the United Nations Economic Commission for Africa.

The new states present some irritating inconsistencies. Observers are occasionally baffled by their difficulty in recognizing Soviet colonialism for what it is. The reasons can be found in the fact that the Soviet Union's conquests are of contiguous territories and the European peoples, in the main, whom they have dominated are not colored.

Some new states wish to become colonial powers on their own. How else can one explain the insistence of Indonesia to annex West New Guinea? India, in her suppression of Hyderabad and refusal to carry through the plebiscite for Kashmir, invoked the same arguments of self-interest frequently used by the older powers.

One must not be disappointed if the nations that have struggled so hard for freedom exhibit a certain arrogance in achieving it, a certain hypocrisy in proclaiming it, and then ape the faults of the older states after having gained it. A European diplomat condemned a new, underprivileged nation for acting as though it were "superior to the rest of mankind." Its leaders, he said, regarded their country as "the only establishment on earth founded on a grand and solid basis," and "the only country embellished with wisdom." His criticism was not directed against any of the very new states. It was the criticism of a Western diplomat lashing out in 1821 at the mixture of moral piety and expansionist policy he saw in the new republic of North America. (Alan F. Westin, *The New York Times*, August 19, 1962.)

The entrance of the new states presents a challenge and an opportunity for the United States. This country struck a blow against the colonial system in 1776. Its revolutionary doctrines, proclaimed by Jefferson, Paine, Lincoln, and Roosevelt, have inspired peoples all over the world to freedom. Now this desire for freedom has reached its climax. Shortly there will be few non-self-governing areas remaining. Most of those capable of full independence will have achieved United Nations membership. The United States should take the lead in developing policies of understanding and helpfulness toward the new members.

The many new states, most of which are uncommitted, could develop into a moral force strong enough to curb the ambitions of the protagonists in the cold war and serve to produce a new type of coexistence.

In the early days of the United Nations, an American Secretary of State remarked that the world had no time for neutral states, that nations were either against us or for us. However, the United States Government now exhibits a more understanding point of view, growing out of its own history.

Secretary of State Dean Rusk, in an address to the National Press Club on July 10, 1961, said:

> We speak of uncommitted nations, and we usually mean those who are committed to neither of the principal blocs on the present scene. But all nations have commitments arising out of their own interests and out of their own hopes for the future. In the United Nations commitments to the Charter can weave the fabric

of common interest which, by reaching beyond the cold war, may determine its outcome.

Undoubtedly, the United Nations faces many problems through its rapidly increasing membership. These are new problems that can be used as steppingstones to a stronger organization.

Fundamentally, the problem of the new states—indeed, that of four-fifths of the nations—is economic and social. They were originally called underprivileged, but now, in more understanding language, are called developing states. These are the states that have little margin of time, leadership, and resources to contribute to the development of world society. Their per capita income is very small. Indeed, 30 per cent of them pay less than 5 per cent of the United Nations budget. Some of them, as has been said earlier, have a richness of historical experience, culture, philosophy, and dignity to contribute to international society.

The vast effort that has so far been made by the United Nations, and the greater effort that must be made, as spelled out in President Kennedy's suggestion of the United Nations Decade of Development, is the subject of the next chapter, "Standards in Larger Freedom."

VII

STANDARDS IN LARGER FREEDOM

A cartoon might picture Father Earth roaming about the celestial bodies, possibly visiting Venus, with Mother Earth shouting to him that there is plenty to do at home. While man is sending satellites into outer space as a prelude to celestial exploration, more than half the people on our planet are hungry, cannot read or write, and are generally in misery. Although the situation may not be very logical, it is quite natural. It is human nature for man to reach for the stars before he solves the problems of poverty about him. If it were not so, the New World would never have been discovered.

The Sixteenth General Assembly dealt both with man's desire to reach the stars and his wish to solve the problem of poverty about him. The late President John F. Kennedy challenged the delegates at that Assembly to extend the United Nations Charter to the area of man's experiments in outer space. He also challenged the delegates to mark the 1960's as the United Nations Decade of Development. The President said that

> the mysteries of outer space must not divert our eyes or our energies from the harsh realities that face our fellow-men. Political sovereignty is but a mockery without the means of meeting poverty, illiteracy and disease. Self-determination is but a slogan if the future holds no hope.

That is why my nation—which has freely shared its capital and its technology to help others help themselves—now proposes officially designating this decade of the 1960's as the United Nations Decade of Development. Under the framework of that resolution, the United Nations' existing efforts in promoting economic growth can be expanded and coordinated.

Since that time, the Secretary-General and the Economic and Social Council have outlined bold plans, with specific goals to be achieved by 1970.

When President Kennedy referred to poverty, illiteracy, and disease, he was referring to the condition of a great part of mankind in what are described as underdeveloped areas. The disproportion of the number of the privileged and the number of the poor of the world was indicated dramatically in the Fourth Special Session of the General Assembly meeting in 1963. In determining the scale by which the members should pay for the upkeep of the military forces in the Congo, the membership of the United Nations was broken down into twenty-seven developed countries and eighty-four less-developed countries.

Paul G. Hoffman, Managing Director of the United Nations Special Fund, has estimated that more than 1.25 billion people live in underdeveloped areas. This figure does not count the more than 650 million people in Red China. One of the most vivid descriptions of these areas is to be found in the excellent booklet written in 1960 by Mr. Hoffman, entitled *One Hundred Countries—One and One-Quarter Billion People*. In it, an underdeveloped country is described as follows:

Everyone knows an underdeveloped country when he sees one. It is a country characterized by poverty, with beggars in the cities, and villagers eking out a bare subsistence in the rural areas. It is a country lacking in factories of its own, usually with inadequate supplies of power and light. It usually has insufficient roads and railroads, insufficient government services, poor communications. It has few hospitals, and few institutions of higher learning. Most of its people cannot read or write. In spite of the generally prevailing poverty of the people, it may have isolated islands of wealth, with a few persons living in luxury. Its banking system is poor; small loans have to be obtained through money lenders who are often little better than extortionists. Another striking characteristic of an underdeveloped country is that its exports to other countries usually consist almost entirely of raw materials, ores or fruits or some staple product with possibly a small admixture of luxury handicrafts. Often the extraction of cultivation of these raw material exports is in the hands of foreign companies.

Mr. Hoffman points out that the United Nations designates as "less developed" all countries and territories in Africa, with the exception of the Union of South Africa; South America, and Asia, with the exception of Japan, Australia, and New Zealand. The United Nations estimates omit mainland China, North Korea, and North Vietnam because of the absence of statistical reports. Of the one and one-quarter billion peoples on which the United Nations had statistics when Mr. Hoffman wrote this report, 70 per cent, or 838 million, had an average per capita annual income of under $100; 208 million had an average per capita annual income of more than $100 but less than $200; 73 million had an average per capita annual income of $200 to $299. The United Nations listed a fourth group, with an average annual income of $300 to $699. It was composed of states that were moving rapidly to escape the designation "less developed." These included Argentina, Lebanon, Puerto Rico, Israel.

Three facts are outstanding in this situation. One is that one and one-quarter billion people, not including Communist China, are miserably poor. The second is that they have been inspired to want a better life. The third is that the members of the United Nations have taken an obligation, individually and collectively, to improve the lot of these people.

Three types of aid are being given to the underprivileged peoples. The largest amount of money, of course, is contributed for the bilateral programs, in which one country gives directly of money and experts to another. The program of the United States, stemming from President Truman's "Point Four" speech, is the largest in terms of money. The contribution of France to technical assistance has been confined primarily to Africa. Her per capita contribution is one of the largest bilateral programs of any of the Great Powers.

Another type of aid is regional, of which the Colombo plan is the best illustration. Through it, the nations of South and Southeast Asia, largely members of the British Commonwealth assisted by the mother country and the United States, have a considerable program of economic development.

For the purpose of discussion here, however, we are concerned with the third type of aid, the multilateral. This is the program of the United Nations and its Specialized Agencies. An effort has been made recently to find a more human phrase than "technical assistance." The word "technical" is hardly broad enough to cover all the investment capital and industrial equipment involved. An effort is also being made to substitute the term "cooperation" for "assistance."

The authority for what has become the vast Technical Assistance Program of the United Nations and its members to help humanity to a better life is to be found in the Charter.

Hugh Keenleyside, of Canada, for twelve years Director of

the United Nations Technical Assistance Program, said that there was abroad in the world a new spirit—a spirit of kindliness. Nations want to help each other, not only because it is to their self-interest to do so, but also because it is the civilized thing to do. Mr. Keenleyside described it as the program based upon a desire to help each other. Today the spirit of the missionary motivates thousands of men and women, from over half the member states of the United Nations, who go into other countries on programs of economic and cultural development.

Technical assistance in some form or other has a long history. The idea that one nation can draw upon the skills of another goes back to antiquity. Christian missionaries were forerunners of technical assistance programs in that they brought medicine, education, and skills to teach people how to live better lives. Those who serve in the United States Peace Corps represent the modern missionary.

The Rockefeller Foundation was an early pioneer in the field of organized philanthropic technical assistance. Much of it was due to the imagination of the late John D. Rockefeller, Jr. The Ford Foundation and other philanthropic bodies have in various ways followed the example set by the Rockefellers.

UN Objectives

To show how the nations have cooperatively responded to the "spirit of kindliness," one has only to look at the program of the United Nations and its various agencies.

It was pointed out in the second chapter that the framers of the United Nations Charter planned a well-rounded organization whose work would provide, on one hand, for the peaceful settlement of disputes and resistance to aggression. On the other hand, it would provide for the removal of the causes of war by promoting human rights and a better eco-

nomic and social life for all people. After the threat of war
has been reduced and the last colony freed, there will remain
as the United Nations' long-range task the promotion of a
better life for the peoples of the earth.

In the Preamble of the Charter, the member nations agree
"to promote social progress and better standards of life in
larger freedom" and "to employ international machinery for
the promotion of the economic and social advancement of all
peoples."

In Chapter IX, Article 55, the United Nations is given
some very considerable authority of its own. Article 55 states:

> With a view to the creation of conditions of stability
> and well-being which are necessary for peaceful and
> friendly relations among nations based on respect for
> the principle of equal rights and self-determination of
> peoples, the United Nations shall promote:
>
> (a) higher standards of living, full employment, and
> conditions of economic and social progress and devel-
> opment;
>
> (b) solutions of international economic, social,
> health, and related problems; and international cul-
> tural and educational cooperation; and
>
> (c) universal respect for, and observance of human
> rights and fundamental freedoms for all without dis-
> tinction as to race, sex, language, or religion.

This is one of the outstanding illustrations of the fact that
the United Nations is more than a league of states—that it has
very considerable authority as an entity.

Article 56 deals with the obligation of the members. It
states: "All Members pledge themselves to take joint and
separate action in cooperation with the Organization for the
achievement of the purposes set forth in Article 55."

The mechanism that would help the United Nations fulfill
these obligations as well as help the members to take joint

and separate action is the Economic and Social Council. It consists of eighteen members of the United Nations elected by the General Assembly. It is responsible to the General Assembly and deals with the broad subjects covered by Article 55. It sets up commissions in the economic and social fields and for the promotion of human rights "and such other commissions as may be required for the performance of its functions." It early established the Commission on Human Rights, the Commission on the Status of Women, and the Social Commission. The Economic and Social Council may coordinate the activities of the Specialized Agencies through consultation and recommendations to these agencies, and through recommendations to the General Assembly and to UN members. Stemming from the Charter and by action of the Economic and Social Council and the Specialized Agencies, a dynamic program has developed.

Despite all of the multilateral and bilateral helpfulness that has been described, the disparity between rich and poor has actually become greater. One hears the statement that "the rich get richer and the poor get poorer." One reason is that the technologically equipped nations are better able to take advantage of modern developments, such as the use of atomic power. At the same time, because of the population explosion, the increased food supply scarcely keeps up with the greater number of people to feed.

The United Nations began with a modest technical assistance program. The inspiration for the American bilateral program, as well as for the UN's expansion of its modest program was President Harry S. Truman's Inaugural Address ("Point Four" speech) on January 20, 1949, in which he said: "We must embark on a bold new program for making the benefits of our scientific advances and industrial progress available for the improvement and growth of underdeveloped areas."

In 1950, the United Nations adopted its Expanded Technical Assistance Program. Three major forms of technical aid are provided: (1) technically qualified experts, sent out at the request of underdeveloped countries to advise governments and train local staff in a wide variety of economic development fields; (2) fellowships or scholarships granted to enable nationals of underdeveloped countries to study modern methods in similar fields abroad, often in conjunction with the sending of an expert; and (3) the organization of training centers and seminars on a regional basis to enable experts of several countries to exchange ideas and experience in particular technical fields. In addition, a limited amount of equipment is provided for demonstration and teaching purposes in support of development projects.

Fifty-four governments pledged slightly over $20 million for the 1950–51 Expanded Technical Assistance Program budget. In contrast, ninety-one governments pledged $118.2 million dollars for the 1964 budget of the Expanded Technical Assistance Program and the Special Fund. The program, therefore, is truly a cooperative effort of many nations, in which the underdeveloped make some contribution even though they will receive the greatest amount of aid. Part of this money is used for the United Nations' own technical assistance program. Part of it is used to pay the Specialized Agencies for undertaking projects. A Technical Assistance Board under the chairmanship of a United Nations staff member contains a representative of each of the Specialized Agencies. They examine requests for aid from member states. The money is contributed to those agencies best able to undertake a particular project.

In order to show how many agencies may cooperate in a broad program, one might use as an example the experience of an American recently returned from a United Nations technical assistance assignment in the Middle East. He had a team of persons working for him, only 10 per cent of whom had come from the United States. Together they faced the following problems: There was the immediate problem of a food supply. The population was growing. What was the best diet for its people based upon what they could best raise? The health of the people was important. If malaria was eliminated, more people could raise more food. What were the best routes by which to get material to market and to the ports for export? The people in the villages badly needed basic education. They must understand more about the tools that were being provided them; they must be able to read the instructions. Their national accounting system was inadequate. Altogether, six agencies of the United Nations combined to help a proud and courageous people, who have demonstrated their willingness to fight for freedom, develop economic and social strength.

In 1958, the creation of the Special Fund added a new dimension to the Technical Assistance Program. The basic purpose of the Fund is to make a survey of the resources of the world and the possibilities of economic development. The experts who direct the program of the Special Fund believe that the two greatest barriers to progress in the underdeveloped areas are inadequate knowledge of basic resources and a shortage of skilled manpower and technical know-how to use these resources effectively. The program of the Special Fund is devoted to these two general lines of study. It undertakes "to reveal and assess the development possibilities of mineral deposits, forests, under-utilized lands and rivers which can provide irrigation, transport and power." Believing that no resource of a country is as important as its human resource, the Special Fund attempts to proceed with advanced education and training programs and research into new and better uses of local manpower. To meet the urgent shortages of trained personnel at all levels, the

Special Fund is helping to establish or strengthen 123 technical training and advanced educational institutes in the low-income countries. These will continue to make a permanent contribution to a country's human resources long after the Special Fund assistance has been withdrawn. Up to the middle of 1963, more than twenty thousand men and women had participated in its formal training programs.

The Special Fund works with and through the Specialized Agencies. It is not its purpose to make outright grants to nations but rather to pay for training projects or surveys that can put people to work and attract outside capital.

Two surveys, one of Argentina's transport and power and another of the Mekong River in Thailand, which together cost $5 million, have alone attracted $385 million of domestic and external capital investment. A central mining-research station in India is facilitating the introduction of new techniques for ensuring safety, health, and efficiency in Indian mines. For this program the International Labor Organization financed the purchase of $675,000 worth of technical and scientific equipment. As a result, research operations are now being carried out in scores of mines. It was possible to reopen a closed mine, employing three thousand workers.

The Specialized Agencies

There are fifteen intergovernmental agencies related to the United Nations. Ten of them participate in the United Nations Technical Assistance Program. In addition to having their programs and budgets, they cooperate in projects of the Expanded Technical Assistance Program and the Special Fund. The other five intergovernmental agencies that are not part of the Special Fund activities have a very important role in helping advance international and national development.

The popular term that is applied to most of these intergovernmental agencies is "Specialized Agencies." Together they touch every phase of human existence outside of political and legal matters. The United Nations family grew in a rather haphazard manner. Some of these agencies antedate the UN, came along with it, or have been developed since to fill a new-found need. President Franklin D. Roosevelt believed that various agencies of the United Nations should be widely scattered. He felt that it would increase knowledge and support of the UN if there were many of its agencies throughout the world.

Some of the Specialized Agencies grew out of the League of Nations or other pre-Second World War years. The oldest, of course, is the International Postal Union.

Space does not permit an analysis of the Specialized Agencies. A book could be written on the history of each one. However, they may be grouped into three divisions: the best-known agencies in the field of human welfare; agencies of a scientific and technological nature which are yet to reach their full development; agencies essentially economic and financial.

Of the first group, the International Labor Organization, the Food and Agriculture Organization, the World Health Organization and the United Nations Educational, Scientific and Cultural Organization are the best known. It is interesting that each of these organizations thinks of world peace in terms of its particular sphere of interest. This makes for a richness and variety of effort.

ILO

The International Labor Organization was an integral part of the League of Nations. It survived the Second World War intact, in exile in Montreal, then returned to Geneva. Its constitution states that world peace is dependent on international social and economic justice. The original purpose of the ILO was to bring together employees, employers, and governments in an effort to improve labor standards by international agreement. The lowest labor standards were by international agreement to be brought nearer and nearer to the standards of the more prosperous nations. The ILO was one of the first international bodies to bring together representatives of private bodies on an equal level with representatives of government. The work of the ILO has shifted considerably to the development of trained and protected workers, the promotion of labor-management cooperation and the freedom of association in the developing countries.

FAO

The Food and Agriculture Organization actually came into being on October 16, 1945, eight days before the UN formally came into being. The FAO grew out of the United Nations Conference on Food and Agriculture, which met at Hot Springs, Virginia, in May, 1943. It has taken the place of the old International Institute of Agriculture in Rome, and is located in that city.

The FAO's contribution is to help people produce more and better food and to distribute it. Officials of the FAO believe that to eliminate hunger is its contribution to peace. The magnitude of the task of this organization is indicated in the statement in the UN publication *The United Nations Family* that hunger "is a bitter and brutal fact to more than half of the world's population"—over three billion people. If the population explosion continues, by the end of the century there will be at least six billion, if not seven billion, people on the earth. The FAO has been helping nations increase their food supply, and so rapid has been the increase in population that it has just about kept up with it. The FAO is teaching nations how to increase the use of arable land, how to recover lands that are worn out from overuse, how to use fertilizers, how to irrigate land and control floods, how to increase the production of fish (one of the best and cheapest sources of animal protein), and so on.

FAO launched the Freedom From Hunger campaign in July, 1960. The campaign was accelerated in October, 1960, when the world's attention was focused on the problem of hunger by a resolution passed in the United Nations General Assembly. As a result, a world food-program, run jointly by the FAO and the United Nations, was set up with an initial working fund of $100 million in cash and commodities.

The organization is governed by a Conference composed of representatives of all the member states.

WHO

The World Health Organization, established on September 1, 1948, in Geneva, is an outgrowth of the League of Nations Health Organization. Its constitution states that the health of all people is fundamental to peace and security and is dependent on the fullest cooperation of individuals and states.

In some ways, the program of the World Health Organization is the best known and best advertised of any of the Specialized Agencies. There are countries in which a majority of the people have seen the United Nations car with the blue insignia and the doctors and nurses with UN armbands engaged in health projects. In some areas every house was sprayed with DDT to eliminate malaria-breeding mosquitoes. *The United Nations Family* says: "Fifteen years of international health work have laid solid grounds for believing that age-old diseases such as malaria, smallpox and yaws can be not only controlled but eradicated—completely wiped out." The organization believes that the goal can be reached, however, only if more and more health workers can be trained, and only if determined campaigns are waged until the last source of infection is destroyed.

It is not an exaggeration to say that there is, in a sense, a race between these two organizations—the FAO and the WHO. Can the food supply of the world keep even with the increasing population, which is partially the result of the success of doctors and health experts in reducing the high mortality rate as a result of disease? However, if people are in better health they can work harder and produce more food. In one area in Pakistan, the elimination of the malaria-breeding mosquitoes resulted in a 100 per cent increase in the rice crop because more people were able to work.

UNESCO

The United Nations Educational, Scientific, and Cultural Organization, which came into being on November 4, 1946, is a successor to the League of Nations Institute of Intellectual Cooperation. The Institute's home was in Paris; consequently, UNESCO is located there. UNESCO's constitution states that wars begin in the minds of men. Therefore, it thinks of war as a result of ignorance. Because it deals with the realm of the intellect, its programs have seemed diffuse and sometimes too intellectual to practical people. In the last few years, however, UNESCO has begun to find itself involved in the broad program of technical assistance. To put it very simply indeed, how can people use the tools given them unless they can understand the instructions that accompany them? UNESCO is therefore concentrating to a very great extent on basic education. The Director-General of UNESCO, returning from Latin America in the spring of 1960, said that UNESCO had succeeded in changing the system of basic education in some Latin American countries.

UNESCO produced a human and instructive documentary film. The opening scenes show a Thai boy riding on his elephant and a Mexican boy riding on his donkey. The boys are very much alike in their simple desires for friendliness and fun. Despite different civilizations and historical backgrounds, the problems of disease and poverty and illiteracy were about the same. One might say that in the overall technical assistance program the ILO infuses social conscience and UNESCO a thirst for knowledge.

Three agencies concern themselves with modern scientific problems: the International Atomic Energy Agency (IAEA), the International Telecommunication Union (ITU), and the World Meteorological Organization (WMO).

IAEA

The International Atomic Energy Agency is one of the most important in the technical and scientific group. President Dwight D. Eisenhower in a dramatic speech to the UN General Assembly in 1953 outlined a program called Atoms for Peace. Deploring the fact that nations had not succeeded in reducing the danger of atomic destruction, the President said he thought it might be helpful if some attention was given to the use of atomic energy for peaceful purposes. As a result, long negotiations took place for the establishment of an appropriate agency, which was finally set up on July 29, 1957, and located in Vienna.

The beginnings of the agency were confused and inauspicious. At the Tenth General Assembly the representatives of the United Kingdom and the United States reported that a committee meeting in Washington had produced a plan for an atomic energy agency, which the United States Government had just published. Members of the United Nations were invited to send their comments and suggestions to Washington. The British Delegate went so far as to say that his country did not believe that the General Assembly was the place to debate as highly technical a subject as atomic energy. Whereupon the General Assembly proceeded to debate both the subject and the plan. Small states felt that their collective judgment expressed through the General Assembly would carry more weight than a series of individual opinions expressed to Washington. The General Assembly functioned at its best and succeeded in modifying the wishes of the Great Powers. When the IAEA was finally established, it had a more intimate relationship to the United Nations than that of the Specialized Agencies.

The Agency was to have several main purposes. It was to act as a bank of fissionable material for the nations that needed it. It was to inspect materials that one nation contributed to another to prevent diversion for military purposes. Inspection was to take place without the veto. The Agency was to establish uniform safeguard and health stand ards in the use of atomic energy.

The prospect of the application of atomic energy to peaceful uses was hailed as the beginning of a second industrial revolution, in which atomic energy would be used for the benefit of mankind while avoiding the unfortunate social and human consequences of the first industrial revolution.

But the Agency has not functioned, as originally planned, as a bank of fissionable material because there continues to be a surplus of conventional power. However, there is concern that some of the sources of conventional power might be exhausted and that atomic energy would be a source of power among the underprivileged as well as the privileged countries in the near future.

As for inspection: unfortunately, the Great Powers did not move immediately to enable the Agency to perform its original function in this regard. As a result, the Agency got off to a shaky start. The United States Government had made over forty bilateral arrangements outside the Agency, the British had made ten, and the Russians fifteen. It is true that many of these arrangements were made before the Agency was completed. However, the Government of the United

States gave the impression, at least, that if the General Assembly accepted the principle of inspection without the veto, the United States would bring its bilateral agreements under the Agency. For a time, it did not move to do so.

In the beginning, therefore, the principal work of the Agency was to develop fellowship and technical assistance programs, various research projects, and a series of scientific and technical conferences. However, in 1962 the Agency began to come into its own and to fulfill its original functions.

The Chairman of the United States Atomic Energy Commission, in an address on September 25, 1963, to the Seventh General Conference of the International Atomic Energy Agency, said, "My Government has made a policy decision to negotiate for the transfer of its bilateral safeguards responsibilities to the Agency." And he pointed out that the United States had placed four of its own reactors under Agency safeguards. He expressed the hope that eventually most countries having nuclear power plants will have the Agency safeguards and that many of them will acquire their nuclear materials through the Agency. The Agency has before it not only the task of developing standards for health and for handling the safe transport of radioactive material, but even the problem of the disposal of radioactive waste matter.

On September 30, 1963, the General Conference of the International Atomic Energy Agency noted with approval a proposal to extend the Agency's safeguards systems to apply to all types and sizes of nuclear-power reactors. The pertinent resolution was approved by a vote of 57 to 4, with the Soviet Union and the United States voting favorably. The statement of the Chairman of the United States Atomic Energy Commission quoted above will go far in nullifying the objection of the nations receiving reactors from the United States that it insists on Agency safeguards for those reactors but no Agency inspection for those in the United States.

Suddenly the Great Powers are returning to the original purposes of the Agency.

The United Nations family contains four Specialized Agencies of a highly technical nature. Their service is universal—they benefit both the privileged and underprivileged nations. Two of them are:

ITU

The International Telecommunication Union, whose work goes back to 1865, is designed, among other things, to extend international cooperation for the improvement and rational use of long-distance communications and to make modern communications widely available. Its home is in Geneva.

A new field is now open to it in the conquest of outer space. Its new responsibilities in this field were formally recognized in the resolution on the peaceful uses of outer space unanimously adopted by the General Assembly on December 20, 1961. It is now engaged in studies of space communication, techniques, and regulations.

WMO

One of the first tasks of the World Meteorological Organization, established in Geneva in 1951, was to arrange for the international exchange of weather reports and to maintain the greatest possible standardization in these reports. Every day, one hundred thousand weather observations for the surface of the earth and ten thousand relating to the upper air are transmitted by stations, aircraft, and ships.

The WMO also helps underdeveloped countries set up national weather services; it seeks to fill gaps in the worldwide network of observing and reporting stations. It studies the role of atomic energy in meteorology. As in the case of the ITU, the adventure into outer space has given the WMO a new task. The United Nations program calls upon the organization in collaboration with the scientific community to develop an international service program for weather observation service forecasting and an international research program to yield greater knowledge of the atmosphere.

Financial Assistance

Five United Nations agencies are concerned with the question of financial assistance. Such assistance covers a wide range, from the hard business loans of the International Bank to the soft loans of the International Development Association. While much of the financial assistance of these agencies is directed at the underdeveloped countries, some of their programs have been of assistance to the United States, Great Britain, and other comparatively prosperous nations.

The International Bank and the International Monetary Fund grew out of a conference at Bretton Woods, New Hampshire, which was held during the Second World War. Its articles of agreement came into force in 1945.

The purpose of the International Bank, called the World Bank, is to lend money to governments and, with governmental guarantees, to governmental agencies and private borrowers for sound projects that assure the repayment of the loans. The World Bank is the toughest of the Specialized Agencies. The Bank's loan funds come in part from members' subscriptions to capital shares. As of June, 1963, the Bank had 85 members. As of the same date it had made 349 loans in 64 countries or territories, aggregating $6,983,-000,000.

The International Monetary Fund works to ensure that different currencies will be convertible, that exchange rates will be stable, and that all countries will have foreign currencies needed for international trade. It consults with governments to provide a procedure for an orderly adjustment of exchange rates. It specifies that any major changes in exchange practices are to be submitted to international consultation. Seventy of the members have established a par value for their currency in consultation with the Fund.

The Fund maintains a currency pool from which a member government may purchase foreign exchange, paying with its own currency. Its help may well be to one of its most prosperous members. It was announced on November 7, 1964, that the so-called "Group of Ten," which arranged three years earlier to lend up to $6 billion to the Fund if the need arose, had agreed to extend $1 billion to Great Britain because of her balance-of-payments crisis. The ten are the United States, Britain, Canada, France, West Germany, Italy, Belgium, The Netherlands, Sweden, and Japan.

The nations were aware of a gap between technical assistance and the conservative loans of the World Bank. Under the technical assistance program of the United Nations and its Specialized Agencies, experts are sent to advise countries on the improvement of their economy, to study their transportation, to show them how to drain their swamps, to inoculate their babies, and to spray their homes to eliminate malaria. What seemed to be needed to fill the gap was financial assistance for basic development projects. These projects are not self-liquidating and cannot justify loans from the World Bank or private investment. But they are so basic that without them underdeveloped countries may never be far enough advanced to justify bank loans and private investment.

The majority of less-developed states have for years advocated a Special United Nations Fund for Economic Development. It became known as SUNFED. The Western powers, particularly the United States and Great Britain, said that they could not contribute to such a fund until they could save money from disarmament. Also, they doubted the soundness of the way SUNFED was to operate.

Alternative approaches have been created to meet the problem. One is the Special Fund, which has already been discussed. The other is the International Development Association (IDA). It is a division of the World Bank. Its purposes are "to promote economic development, increase productivity and thus raise standards of living in the less developed areas of the world. . . ." This is done by making loans on more flexible terms than the conventional loans of the World Bank.

Membership in the IDA is open to the same countries that are members of the World Bank. As of mid-1963, 75 countries had joined. The more highly developed member countries pay their subscriptions over a five-year period in gold or freely convertible currencies. The less-developed member nations pay only 10 per cent of their subscriptions in gold or freely convertible currencies; 90 per cent is paid in their own currencies. By the end of June, 1963, the IDA had extended 38 development credits in 18 countries, totaling $490 million.

The purpose of the International Finance Corporation (IFC) is to assist in financing industrial enterprises. It deals with private citizens and corporations rather than with governments. It provides risk capital and makes its investments in private enterprise under governmental guarantee.

Special Bodies

The United Nations family contains, in addition to the Specialized Agencies, three special bodies. They are the United Nations Children's Fund, the Office of the United Nations High Commissioner for Refugees and the United Nations Relief and Works Agency.

The Children's Fund (UNICEF) began as an emergency organization. When its continuing need was recognized, it was established as a permanent body. It has succeeded in feeding millions of children and giving them medical assistance. UNICEF is financed in part by private citizens through such programs as the purchase of greeting cards. It is one of the few United Nations programs that has financial participation by individuals.

The United Nations High Commissioner for Refugees is trying to keep ahead of the number of refugees, but man's inhumanity to man produces them about as fast as the older ones can be settled. World Refugee Year, which ran from July 1, 1959, through June 30, 1960, may have accomplished much to focus the attention of the world on the seriousness of the refugee problem. It encouraged people to contribute money for the clearing of more camps. The problem of European refugees was almost solved at the end of World Refugee Year; most of the camps in Europe have been reduced or closed. But the number of refugees increases in Asia and Africa.

In 1949, the General Assembly established the United Nations Relief and Works Agency for Palestine refugees in the Near East. In 1948, hundreds of thousands of Palestinian Arabs became refugees as a result of the hostilities between Arab states and Israel. Because of the increase of births over deaths, the number of refugees has grown to about 1,200,000. UNRWA, the United Nations Relief and Works Agency, is a special temporary, nonpolitical agency which, in cooperation with the countries in which the refugees are housed, provides basic rations, health, and welfare services for many of the refugees. It provides education and training. The word *temporary* should be emphasized. The refugees must eventually become absorbed into the countries where they are now located and become economic assets to these countries.

Coordination

How much coordination should there be between the United Nations and its Specialized Agencies? This is an increasingly important problem. The agencies are highly autonomous. There is obviously an advantage in having separate agencies in that each brings experts from a particular field. The total result is a richness of personal contributions. However, there would seem to be need of increasing coordination in order to make a massive assault on the problems of the underprivileged. A further challenge came through the United Nations Decade of Development program.

The late Secretary-General Dag Hammarskjöld, in his address dedicating the buildings of the University of Chicago Law School on May 1, 1960, pointed out two tendencies. One was the desire to create a new organization for each task undertaken by the United Nations. Perhaps the process of proliferation will stop with an agency for outer space—and one for world trade. The time may have come to strengthen existing machinery rather than to create new bodies.

The second tendency pointed out by Mr. Hammarskjöld was that of each agency to be quite independent in its relationship with the others. At the same time, most members of the Agencies are also members of the United Nations, and most of them contribute to the Technical Assistance and Special Fund programs. The Secretary-General, referring to this independent relationship, went on to say: "At least it seems to me that, if this tendency is accepted and continued, it should be counterbalanced by an effort to evolve new forms for integration of the work of the various international agencies."

Another agency of the United Nations, the General Agreement on Tariffs and Trade (GATT), grew out of an international commercial treaty negotiated between some of the members. It has developed a secretariat and, in a sense, it functions as an international trade organization is supposed to function. According to Richard Gardner in his book *In Pursuit of World Order*, "GATT now serves the free world in four principal ways: as a forum for negotiations on the reduction of tariffs and other trade barriers; as a set of trade rules governing the conduct of trade policy; as an instrument for the interpretation of these rules and the adjustment of differences; and as a vehicle for developing and articulating new trade policy. Each of these functions is important in the current effort to clear the channels of world trade."

In the spring of 1964, an international trade conference was held in Geneva. It was the largest intergovernmental conference ever assembled. Representatives from 119 states participated. This conference was notable because the major tensions were not East-West ones but rather North-South. In other words, the tensions between the comparatively wealthy industrialized nations of the north and the underprivileged low-income group of raw-material states of the south provided the fundamental clash of interests at the Conference. The differences were not those of cold war and ideologies, but rather differences of economics. As Secretary-General U Thant said:

> Now we know that the South can be identified as a large group of more than 75 votes, when it chooses to assert itself. In demonstrating such a possibility, the Conference may have signalled a turn in the history of international economic relations. The contribution that may be expected of the 75 to the solution of world problems will depend to a great degree upon the validity of my faith in the unique value of the United Nations as an instrument for reconciling differences of opinion and not only as a framework in which they can manifest themselves.

The Conference recommended action by the General Assembly to attain two goals: (1) to enlarge the role of the United Nations in the field of international trade; and (2) "to add to the broad concepts of negotiation and cooperation inherent in the Charter new conciliation procedures which are essential to carry out decisions whose ultimate purpose is to change the existing international division of labor." Following these recommendations, the Nineteenth General Assembly established a permanent International Trade Conference as part of the United Nations' machinery.

Regional Economic Commissions

The United Nations has created four regional economic commissions: one for Asia and the Far East (1947), one for Europe (1947), one for Latin America (1948), and one for Africa (1958).

The Commission for Africa has had a particularly serious challenge because of the rapidity with which a great part of Africa became free. The Commission for Africa has thirty-four members: the thirty-three African states that are members of the United Nations and Portugal. The Commission also has ten associate members, some of which will become full members. The main tasks of the Commission are to promote and facilitate concerted action for the economic development of Africa, including its social aspects, with a view to raising the standard of living and the level of economic activity. Further, it is to strengthen and maintain the economic relations of the various countries and territories of Africa, both among themselves and with other countries of the world.

To return to the introductory paragraphs of this chapter, it is evident that the General Assembly of 1961 was one of the UN's most productive assemblies. It accepted both the challenge of a program in outer space and the Decade of Development, with its goal materially to advance the standards of the underprivileged by 1970.

Following the adoption by the Sixteenth General Assembly of the Decade of Development program, the General Assembly prepared an outline of problems that were submitted to the next session of the Economic and Social Council. Almost five years, almost half the decade, have passed. The next edition of this series—the United Nations of the first twenty-five years—will measure how far the nations have come in achieving the goal of the Decade of Development. Success will not only mean an improvement in the lives of the underprivileged peoples of the world and greater opportunities for the minority of the privileged. It also will mean that many of the tensions leading to political unrest will have been removed.

It has been pointed out that the part of the United Nations program dealing with economic and social matters receives but 5 per cent of the publicity given to the United Nations. The public is most interested in the drama of crisis, threats, and fighting. But in the long run what the United Nations is able to do to promote economic and social well-being may be the deciding factor for world peace.

VIII

STRENGTHENING THE UNITED NATIONS

The startling changes that have come to the world since the Second World War ended foretell even more startling changes to come. Man looks into a future of outer space travel and is planning to land on celestial bodies. His population is increasing so rapidly that he contemplates harvesting crops from the sea.

These changes dictate an ever stronger United Nations. In twenty years, it has grown to become a much larger organization and in some ways a much stronger organization than the UN of 1946. It must continue to grow.

The word "stronger" must necessarily concern every phase of United Nations activity. It means more precise law to govern the relations between peoples of the world. It means a vast amount of machinery for adjustment of ever more difficult problems. It includes the possibility of the United Nations assuming sovereignty and administering authority in some areas, such as outer space and the bed of the sea beyond the continental shelf.

So far, the United Nations has developed by improvisation; constantly meeting unanticipated challenges; gaining strength by doing; constantly developing and using executive and legislative power.

It may be that the United Nations must develop this way. Undoubtedly it must add increasingly sovereign power as the immediate need demands; in fact, the United Nations must act as a limited government—if the world is to have peace it has no other choice.

The process of improvisation may well continue until the nations accept a plan for total disarmament. Such an acceptance would include specific plans for strengthening the United Nations peace machinery, based upon world law, with an international police force. Obviously, when that moment comes, the nations must know more precisely what guarantees their international society will give them in return for disarmament.

At the moment, the United Nations is in a shadowy area between a league of states and a world government. Indeed, this was implied in an advisory opinion of the International Court of Justice in 1949.

In 1948, the General Assembly authorized the Secretary-General to ask for an advisory opinion as to whether the United Nations had the authority to claim damages from member or nonmember states for losses suffered by its personnel in their territories. The losses in Palestine had been quite serious. In 1949, the Court in an advisory opinion described the nature of the United Nations in such a manner that the late A. H. Feller, Chief Counsel to the United Nations, compared the opinion to the famous *McCulloch* vs. *Maryland* decision, which was very influential in United States constitutional history. After reviewing the obligations imposed upon the members, the International Court of Justice decided:

> In the opinion of the Court, the Organization was intended to exercise and enjoy, and is in fact exercising and enjoying, functions and rights which can only be explained on the basis of the possession of a large

measure of international personality and the capacity to operate upon an international plane. It is at present the supreme type of international organization, and it could not carry out the intentions of its founders if it was devoid of international personality. It must be acknowledged that its Members, by entrusting certain functions to it, with the attendant duties and responsibilities, have clothed it with the competence required to enable those functions to be effectively discharged.

The Court concluded that to say the organization has "a large measure of international personality" is not the same as saying that the United Nations is a state; still less is it the same thing as saying it is a superstate.

Here, then, is the United Nations, an international personality, clothed by its framers with authority to operate on an international plane and whose members have taken important obligations toward it. But it is neither a state nor a superstate. This dilemma is inherent in the development of world society.

Opposing Theories of Membership

Two opposing theories of membership were considered before the San Francisco Conference and are compromised in the Charter. One was the idea of a universal organization to which all nations would automatically belong. The other was that of an organization to which "peace-loving" states would be admitted.

The thought that the United Nations might be a universal organization based on law entered the discussion in Washington in a committee of five,* meeting under the chairmanship of Sumner Welles, which undertook the first United States

* This committee of private citizens met at the State Department in 1942-43. It was composed of James T. Shotwell, Isaiah Bowman, Hamilton Fish Armstrong, Benjamin V. Cohen and Clark M. Eichelberger.

draft of a United Nations charter. A working paper submitted to the Welles committee by the author of this book stated: "The United Nations might be compared to some individuals in the frontier community who have acted as vigilantes to suppress lawlessness. While they are suppressing such lawlessness they have decided to establish a reign of law and order with means of law enforcement and obligations of good behavior binding upon all nations whether they wish to consent or not."

As a result of this philosophy, the draft of the Welles committee contained the following paragraphs:

"1. The membership of the International Organization shall reflect the universal character of the international community.

"2. All qualified states and dominions shall be members of the International Organization. The Council shall decide as to the nature of the qualifications."

Presumably all states that were members of the family of nations automatically were to belong to the United Nations. True, the Council was to decide upon the nature of the qualifications, but the qualifications were understood to be technical, such as what constitutes a state. Qualifications of good conduct were not involved.

This was the concept of universal membership. All nations were to be bound by the Charter. There could be no escape. A nation could be denied the benefits of the community because of aggression, as an individual is denied the benefits of his community if he is guilty of an offense. But the idea of admission, expulsion, and withdrawal from the rule of law was not recognized.

Unfortunately, from the writer's point of view, the Department of State rejected the concept of universality in favor of standards of good conduct. Excluding Charter members, Article 4 (1) provides: "Membership in the United

Nations is open to all other peace-loving states which accept the obligations contained in the present Charter and, in the judgment of the Organization, are able and willing to carry out these obligations." Consequently, a nation may apply; it may be admitted; it may be rejected; and it may be expelled.

Only one aspect of the original concept of universality based on law remains in the Charter: Article 2 (6) provides: "The Organization shall ensure that states which are not Members of the United Nations act in accordance with these Principles so far as may be necessary for the maintenance of international peace and security."

The United Nations can be strengthened in a number of ways. Its present strength is due to the use of a number of them.

The first is by a more loyal and imaginative fulfillment of their obligations by the member states. This fulfillment is the subject of the last chapter.

Other means by which the United Nations can be or has been expanded and strengthened are:

· By a liberal interpretation of the Charter.

· By the expansion of existing machinery and the addition of new bodies as the need is revealed.

· By having administrative authority in those areas not under national sovereignty, such as outer space.

· By a constant approach toward universality.

· By having an independent source of income.

· By improving the structure and functioning of existing bodies.

· By the development of the processes of world law, and by a greater use of the International Court of Justice.

· By the revision of the text of the Charter.

Liberal Versus Strict Constructionists

The liberal interpretation of the United Nations Charter reminds one of early American constitutional history. The strict constructionists have asserted that the bodies of the United Nations could do nothing that was not spelled out in the Charter. The liberal constructionists have been willing that the United Nations assume, by agreement of an appropriate number of its members, such authority as is necessary to fulfill the purposes of the organization as defined in the language of the Charter.

The Soviet Union has led the strict constructionist bloc so far as the political and security articles of the Charter are concerned. It has objected to the increasing use of the General Assembly at the expense of the Security Council. Practically everything undertaken by the General Assembly that seems to be at the expense of the Security Council is to the Soviet Union illegal. It objected to the Uniting for Peace Resolution and abstained on the establishment of UNEF. The Soviet Union would use the General Assembly as a propaganda organ but not for action—that it would leave to the Security Council.

Article 2 (7) is one of the articles that have been a source of debate between the strict and liberal constructionists. This article provides: "Nothing contained in the present Charter shall authorize the United Nations to intervene in matters which are essentially within the domestic jurisdiction of any state . . ." Here, the colonial powers are the strict constructionists. Most of them have felt that the General Assembly has gone too far in supporting the independence of colonial peoples.

Fortunately, in critical days there has usually been at least a two-thirds majority of the members of the United Nations who supported a liberal construction of the Charter. At any particular moment, the majority has been willing that the organization grow and expand to meet the needs of the time. During most of the life of the United Nations, the United States has been numbered among the liberal constructionists.

The Expansion of Existing Machinery and the Addition of New Bodies

As has been seen in Chapter VII the various agencies of the United Nations have increased until they number sixteen. In addition, many commissions, committees, bodies of all kinds, both temporary and permanent, have been created as the needs require.

Three new agencies may be on the horizon. The vast vista of man's explorations in outer space opening before him may prompt an agency in that field. There was considerable discussion at the United Nations World Trade Conference at Geneva in 1964 that an international trade organization should be set up.

The possibility of a disarmament organ so broad in scope as to be a new security agency of the United Nations is discussed later in this chapter.

The new agencies, while part of the United Nations system, will vary greatly in constitutional structure.

By Having Administrative Authority in Those Areas Not Under National Sovereignty, Such as Outer Space

One of the most effective ways of giving the United Nations strength would be to give it sovereign authority in areas where no nation has extended its own sovereign claims. There are three such areas: part of Antarctica; the bed of the sea beyond the continental shelf; and outer space.

As for the first, the nations have moved to prevent Antarctica from being cut up by sovereign claims or used for military purposes. The nations that have explored in Antarctica at a conference in Washington in 1959 agreed to a program of cooperation for the development of this area. Both the United States and the Soviet Union have refused to recognize new territorial claims by others made in the area. It would not take too much imagination to establish the principle of United Nations sovereignty in Antarctica.

As for the bed of the sea beyond the continental shelf, there is danger that nations will try to mark off vast areas of the sea to preserve exclusive fishing rights, to explore resources, and to find crops of food that might be harvested from the sea. Extensive exploration for oil is now going on in the shallow North Sea.

Under the guise of military necessity, the tradition of freedom of the seas has been violated in rather a large way by several of the Great Powers. At times they have ordered world shipping to avoid large areas of the Pacific Ocean where nuclear or missile tests were to take place.

The world may be facing another era of territorial expansion, accompanied by rivalries, counterclaims, and armed conflict. And, of course, a few of the Great Powers would have the capacity to undertake such development or to conquer such areas, freezing out the smaller states.

An expansion of United Nations sovereignty to outer space would seem to be particularly pressing. Certainly the present inadequate doctrine of freedom of the seas should not be a precedent for a doctrine of freedom of outer space. Many wars have been fought over freedom of the seas. The nations cannot afford even one war to assure the freedom of the heavens.

In 1958, the then Senator Lyndon B. Johnson appeared before the United Nations General Assembly to propose the creation of the United Nations *ad hoc* Committee on the Peaceful Uses of Outer Space. That committee in its report pointed out a developing international tragedy. Many states that would like to participate in the adventure to the heavens must stand idly by while two space giants make the great adventure. It concluded with the statement that "space activities must to a large extent be an effort of Planet Earth as a whole." This was probably the first time that Planet Earth was spoken of as a political unit.

Although the United Nations has not yet extended its sovereignty to outer space, it has already moved some considerable distance to reduce the possibility of anarchy in outer-space exploration. In history's most remarkable extension of world law, the General Assembly in 1961 proclaimed that the principles of the Charter and international law were binding in the area of man's experiments in outer space. It further proclaimed that while outer space and celestial bodies are free for exploration and use by all states in conformity with international law, they are not subject to national appropriation. A resolution in the Assembly in 1963 forbade nations from carrying atomic weapons on outer-space vehicles.

The Eighteenth General Assembly unanimously adopted the Declaration of Legal Principles Governing the Activities of States in the Exploration and Use of Outer Space. The Declaration contained nine principles.

Fortunately, an effort is being made to enable many nations to share the blessings and the adventure of outer space development. U Thant points out, "It is gratifying that, through the United Nations, countries at the most varied levels of development are being enabled to work together with the space Powers in a cooperative effort to develop a law of space that will meet the needs of the international community as a whole."

The Committee on the Peaceful Uses of Outer Space, with the assistance of the Secretariat, disseminates information on national and cooperative international space programs and on space-related activities and resources of the United Nations, the Specialized Agencies, and other competent international bodies. The steadily developing World Weather Watch program of the World Meteorological Organization is the kind of program that can be developed for all mankind. The Committee has recommended that United Nations sponsorship be granted to India for the continuing operation of the Thumba Equatorial Sounding Rocket Launching Station. Brazil has informed the Committee that it will ask for United Nations endorsement of the sounding rocket facilities that it is setting up.

By a Constant Approach Toward Universality

Despite the criticism of the size and lack of experience of some of the very new states, the United Nations has been strengthened as it has moved toward universality. In fact, if it is to become a world society based on law all nations must be members of it. One of the weaknesses of the League of Nations was that many parts of the world were in colonial status and could not be represented by governments of their own choosing.

When the author undertook a review of the first ten years of the United Nations, he devoted considerable attention to the devices by which some seventeen applicants had been denied admission to the organization. Indeed, in 1955 the Secretary-General pointed out that less than half of the European states were members. The Soviet Union in the Security Council vetoed the states whose membership was desired by the Western powers. In return, the Western powers by a process of abstentions and negative votes made it impossible to secure a council majority of seven for the admission of those states proposed by the Soviet Union. Such conduct did little credit to either power.

The Canadian Delegation in the Tenth General Assembly, almost singlehandedly succeeded over the objections of some of the Great Powers in breaking the logjam on membership. Since that time, the membership has grown to 114; 125 is predicted within a few years. Instead of attempting to keep each others' friends out of the United Nations, it seems as if the Western powers and the Soviet Union and, of course, the new states recently freed from colonialism seem equally eager to admit any state immediately upon its independence. Usually the colonial power is the first to sponsor the admission of its liberated colony.

Switzerland is not a member of the United Nations. Neither are the three divided states of Germany, Korea, and Vietnam.

The major membership problem is that of China. One-fourth of the population of the world—Communist China—is not represented in the United Nations by the government in effective control. From 1951 to 1962, various nations have asked to have the question of change in Chinese representation placed upon the agenda of the General Assembly. Each time the move was voted down. Beginning in 1963, the item was placed on the agenda, but a motion to expel the Nationalist Chinese delegates and seat the Peking delegates was defeated. Since China is a Charter member of the United Nations, the problem of which delegates should represent China in the United Nations has until recently been considered a procedural matter. However, the issue has been recognized as a major one, requiring a two-thirds vote to solve. This fact, plus the moral dilemma raised by Communist Chinese conduct, assumes such importance that inevitably many people debate the question as if it were a matter of admitting a new state.

One can argue for or against seating the Peking delegates in the United Nations, depending on which theory of membership one supports. Those opposed to seating the Peking delegates assert that Communist China can hardly be called a peace-loving state. Thousands of American homes have memories of sons lost or imprisoned in Korea because of the intervention of Communist China in the Korean fighting. Its government is still technically an aggressor in Korea. It is committing genocide in Tibet. It threatens the frontiers of India. It rejects co-existence and proclaims war as an instrument of national policy. Presumably it would add one more veto in the Security Council. Its voice in the General Assembly would be a strident one.

Those arguing for the seating of the Peking delegates say that the United Nations should be a reflection of the world as it is. The lawless should be brought within the law. It should be a universal organization. Communist China contains one-quarter of the population of the world. Many problems of the Pacific area cannot be solved without her participation. American government officials recognize that agreements for disarmament would be meaningless without Peking's participation.

The one proposal that seems acceptable to a considerable majority of the members of the United Nations is not acceptable to either China. It is a proposal that delegates from both governments be seated on the ground that each claims to speak for China, which is a Charter member. Many states, particularly those recently admitted, will not vote to expel a member, such as Nationalist China. Indeed, it is a general belief in many circles that the Soviet Union, despite its advocacy of Peking's membership, really does not wish it, or it would not pose the question in a way that many members cannot accept. Should the question be posed as to whether or not both governments should be admitted, there might be an overwhelming favorable response. It would seem that the larger unit would have to be given the permanent seat on the Security Council reserved for China.

The longer the delay, the more difficult it may be to make

satisfactory arrangements for Peking's entrance. In the spring of 1950, when Trygve Lie suggested that the question of China's representation in the United Nations be dealt with, Communist China was not strong. She had just won control of the mainland. She had not committed aggression on her neighbors. She needed aid and friends. But without any help from the West, and aided principally by the Soviet Union, the Peking regime became stronger, more aggressive, and more intractable. In 1950, the Peking Government was anxious to have its delegates seated in the United Nations. Her bitterness has increased as she has been kept out of the family of nations and denounced, particularly by the United States. There is something quite illogical about saying that the Chinese Peoples' Republic must be bound by the obligations of the Charter but should not participate in the work of the organization.

By Independent Source of Income

One of the ways of strengthening the United Nations is to give it an independent source of income. Traditionally, the members are unwilling to give the organization the financial support necessary for it to attain the strength it needs to preserve peace and advance the international good society. Many nations today are so steeped in the war tradition of hundreds of years that they will pay unlimited sums for military preparedness while haggling at a comparatively small sum of money for the strengthening of the United Nations. The fact that the entire annual cost of the United Nations is small incomparison to the cost of present-day battleships or to expenses involved in nuclear development reduces the penury of the members to an absurdity. The lessons of history dictate that the United Nations can only have the necessary sovereign independence and strength by having an independent source of income in addition to the contributions made by the member states.

Where can this independent source of income be found? Possibly by levying a tax on services that the United Nations is performing or on the international development of areas where man's sovereign claims have not been extended. The United Nations is tangibly improving the living standards of various nations of the world. Should not an improvement tax be levied? Twenty boats dot the Atlantic Ocean by arrangement with the International Civil Aviation Organization in order to effect a rescue of a plane at sea. Travelers should be willing to pay a small tax on their tickets to help support this security feature. The World Bank is now contributing some of its surplus to the program of the International Development Association. Could any of its surplus be contributed to the machinery for enhanced political security on the ground that enhanced political security makes it possible for the Bank safely to expand its conservative investments? Should not the United Nations derive a fee from outer space television and telephonic communications? These telephonic communications will eventually be possible because of a very large financial investment by governments and because of the peace and order in outer space that the United Nations advances. The private communication corporations that have been cut into the development of the Telstar program should not be permitted to prevent a portion of the revenue going to the United Nations. If the United Nations takes title to the bed of the sea beyond the continental shelf, should it not be able profitably to license commercial ventures in the area?

By Improving the Structure and Function of Existing Bodies

The United Nations has been improved, as it can be improved, by strengthening the structure and the functions of its existing bodies.

It was pointed out in Chapter II that the crisis over paying peacekeeping assessments under Article 19 has grown to confront the United Nations with a legal and constitutional crisis. Basically, the problem is to preserve the principle of sovereign equality of states and at the same time to recognize power. Each nation, large or small, has one vote in the General Assembly. At the same time, there are some nations in the United Nations that have more power to assist in the functions of the United Nations and more money to contribute to peacekeeping. Speaking to the United Nations Association and its members on December 13, 1964, Mr. Harlan Cleveland, Assistant Secretary of State for International Organization Affairs, said:

> And indeed, the constitutional issues that now face the UN are not so different from those which almost tore our own Constitutional Convention apart, in Philadelphia, nearly two centuries ago. There the problem was how to reconcile the sovereign equality of states in an infant nation, with the fact that some of the states were very small and others were very large.
>
> Here in the United Nations, today, there are two clearly discernible facts which nobody disputes, but which are not easy to combine into one political system: On the one hand the sovereign equality of nations, an immutable principle of the Charter; on the other hand the uneven distribution of real power and real resources in the real world. Somehow the small number of large and powerful countries must come to terms with the sovereign equality of nations. And somehow the small-country majority in the United Nations must come to terms with the minority of nations that make the UN not a debating society but an action agency for peace.

In his address before the Pacem in Terris Convocation, Secretary-General U Thant said on February 19, 1965:

We are now witnessing the beginning of the great debate—whether the big Powers in unison, through the agency of the Security Council, should take exclusive responsibility for maintaining international peace and security while the General Assembly functions as a glorified debating society in political matters, or whether an attempt should be made to secure a fair, equitable, and clearly defined distribution of functions of the two principal organs, in the light of the changing circumstances, and, particularly, bearing in mind the increase in the membership of the Organization, from 50 in 1945 to 114 in 1965. Account will have to be taken of the fact that in the General Assembly are represented, in addition to the big Powers, all the other States, the smaller Powers, whose understanding, assistance and co-operation are nevertheless essential in regard to decisions involving issues of international peace and security. . . .

Chapter II describes how the center of gravity of the United Nations shifted from the Security Council to the General Assembly, beginning with the Uniting for Peace Resolution. The General Assembly assumed responsibilities for peacekeeping when the Security Council was blocked by the veto.

Several factors have led to a reopening of the relationship of these two bodies in the maintenance of international peace and security. The Security Council, within the past few years, has assumed some of the responsibilities that were imposed on it in the Charter. No veto has been cast in the Security Council against the establishment of peacekeeping operations for five years. In 1959 the Security Council held five meetings; in 1964 it held over one hundred meetings. In the case of Cyprus and the confrontation over the Congo, the Security Council functioned decisively. However, one's optimism at this development is tempered by the fact that the cold war again had its chilling effect on Security Council operations. The Soviet indiscriminate support of Indonesia resulted in the Soviet veto of a mild resolution that would have called for the parties (Indonesia and Malaysia) to refrain from all threat or use of force and to respect each other's territorial independence.

As was pointed out in Chapter VI, "The Hot Winds of Freedom," the sudden addition of many new, small and inexperienced states gave rise to doubt as to the capacity of the General Assembly to take action on peacekeeping, as it did in Suez and in the latter days of the Congo.

Obviously a body of eleven men can, if so inclined, discuss a threat to the peace of the world and take action more quickly than the General Assembly. The Soviet Union, and possibly France, if one can correctly interpret General de Gaulle's wishes, would like to re-establish the authority of the Security Council and remove from the General Assembly any peacekeeping responsibilities. On the other hand, the United States, which sponsored the Uniting for Peace Resolution, will not go so far in re-establishing the authority of the Security Council as to deny the right of the General Assembly to take action if the Security Council is paralyzed by the veto.

Furthermore, the small states are not going to give up the rights which they have won for the General Assembly.

Without attempting to anticipate the deliberations of the Committee of Thirty-Three, the writer would predict that a compromise will be found between the authority given to the Security Council in the Charter and the authority assumed by the General Assembly through a liberal interpretation of the Charter to direct peacekeeping operations and collective security. A new system of financing peacekeeping operations might also be found.

It has already been suggested by the Government of the

United States that a committee be set up to arrange for the financing of specific peacekeeping operations. This committee would be weighted in favor of those who would carry a heavy share of the expenses for such operations. The authority cannot be vested entirely in the financially prosperous, however. It must be remembered that so far the small states (with the exception of Britain) have contributed the troops for peacekeeping operations. They will undoubtedly do so in the future. It is worth analyzing the weaknesses and means by which both the Security Council and the General Assembly could be strengthened and their procedures improved.

As for the Security Council, the use of the veto cannot be limited nor that body increased in size without a revision of the text of the Charter. As for the General Assembly, much can be done to improve the efficiency of its operations through decision of its members, because the Assembly is the judge of its own competence and procedure. No Charter changes would be necessary to enhance the effectiveness of the Economic and Social Council, except to increase its size. The Trusteeship Council will gradually fall into disuse as the last trusteeships are liquidated unless given a new kind of authority over some sixty small areas and groups of people that could not constitute viable states.

The Security Council can be the most satisfactory or the most unsatisfactory body imaginable. There have been times when the members of the Security Council sincerely met their responsibilities. The galleries were packed; the newspapermen waited eagerly; statesmen not members of the Security Council stood around the horseshoe table; in fact, the whole world was concentrated on the deliberations of eleven men. These were the great moments. These eleven men were aware of the responsibilities placed upon them in the Charter. These observers felt that the body not only had authority conferred upon it by the Charter but by the membership that stood behind it. Certainly it is easier and more comfortable for eleven men to debate and pass judgment than for the members of the General Assembly to do so.

There have been other times when one veto has frustrated the wish of the rest of the members of the Council. There have been times when to win a point in the cold war seemed more important than reaching agreement. Then the world turned sadly away, convinced that the Security Council did not represent the hopes of the world.

If the Great Powers today were to put aside cold war considerations and take decisions based upon merit, the Security Council, for the present and the immediate future, could fulfill its responsibilities under the Charter.

For the long-time pull the Security Council has serious structural weaknesses. It represents a rigid power structure that will not stand the test of time. The framers of the Charter proceeded on two false assumptions: that five powers could remain united indefinitely; that the five powers so designated would forever be the five on whose unity the success of the organization depended. The power of nations rises and falls like waves of the sea. One of the governments permitted to use the veto in the Security Council, Nationalist China, is a government-in-exile. Who knows which will be the most powerful nations fifty years hence? Nevertheless, the Security Council is so organized that these five Great Powers can veto forever a revision of the Charter that might affect their exclusive dominance.

Other nations will increase in power as time goes on, and they, too, will want representation on the Security Council. Japan and Italy, and eventually Germany, are great power members. Others, such as India, will move rapidly into the same class. The League of Nations Covenant authorized the Council, with the permission of the majority of the Assembly, to add both to its permanent members and to its non-permanent members. However, the United Nations Security Council cannot so increase its members without a revision of the Charter.

Many of the nonpermanent seats on the Security Council are by custom earmarked geographically: two for Latin America, one for the British Commonwealth, one for Western Europe, leaving two seats to be rotated among the other members. The Soviet Union claims that one of the seats was by agreement to be earmarked for Eastern Europe. The United States denies that there was any such "gentlemen's agreement" beyond the first year of the United Nations. However, the disagreement between the two nuclear giants over this point is responsible for several deadlocked votes in the General Assembly.

The Eighteenth General Assembly passed on to the Member States amendments to increase the size of the Security Council to fifteen by adding four nonpermanent members, and the size of the Economic and Social Council to be increased from eighteen to twenty-five members.

The amendments have been ratified by sixty-three States including the Soviet Union. In April, 1965, the President of the United States asked consent of the Senate to the ratification of these amendments.

The ten nonpermanent seats on the Security Council would include five from Africa and Asia, one from Eastern Europe, two from Latin America and two from Western Europe and other areas.

The original American working draft of the Welles committee, which has been referred to, provided that each geographic area should select its member or members to serve on the Security Council. This arrangement has much to recommend it.

Another device that has been suggested for the election

of members to the Security Council is a plan that would be a wide modification of the method of electing judges to the International Court of Justice. A committee of nominees in each member country places not more than four names in nomination, only two of whom may be of their own nationality. The entire list is then voted on by the Security Council and General Assembly sitting simultaneously. The Court statute contains no provision that there must always be a judge from each of the five major powers. Nevertheless, it has worked out that way.

It has been suggested that some such method of electing members of the Security Council might work out satisfactorily. Now, quite obviously, two powers so overshadow the world that they hold the fate of mankind in their atomic stockpiles. Three others, the U.K., France and now China, have joined the atomic club. A Security Council on which these nations were not represented would ignore the power facts of life and could scarcely be responsible for the maintenance of international peace and security. However, power shifts and is relative. Other nations will be capable of assuming the responsibilities imposed upon the Security Council members. A flexible means of electing all of its members should result in an adequate reflection of world power at any moment. The arbitrary distinction between five great powers and all the rest of the members classed as small powers would be abandoned.

Over one hundred so-called small powers may not be content forever to have five powers holding permanent seats in the Security Council and exercising the right of veto in the body that has the primary responsibility for the maintenance of international peace and security. Other nations are going to increase in power as time goes by, and they, too, will want an equal chance to sit on the Security Council. If not, they will attempt to expand the authority of the General Assembly at the expense of the Security Council as they have been doing.

As for the General Assembly, a strengthening of its procedures can be undertaken more quickly than a reorganization of the Security Council. The machinery of this body is capable of wide modification and expansion without any necessary revision of the Charter. Nor is there a rigid veto with which to contend in making changes. Since all the members of the United Nations belong to the General Assembly, they will undertake its reform with greater enthusiasm than a move to strengthen the Security Council, on which so few of them have a chance to serve.

Previous chapters have shown how the General Assembly assumed specific authority for peacemaking. Its moral influence grew. It assumed considerable legislative and executive authority. It disposed of the colonies that Italy surrendered at the close of the war. It partitioned Palestine. It instructed the Secretary-General to establish a United Nations Emergency Force for the Gaza Strip and to recruit a fleet of vessels to clear the Suez Canal. It proclaimed the Uniting for Peace Resolution. It adopted the Universal Declaration of Human Rights and the declaration of independence for colonial areas. It extended the law of the Charter and international law to outer space and agreed that nations will not carry nuclear weapons on outer space vehicles.

If the United Nations is to gather increasing strength to fulfill its tasks, it is inevitable that the General Assembly will be the parliament of nations. It will be the place where the hopes and the protests of the nations can be expressed. As it approaches universality, it will be the spokesman for approximately 125 members. It can evolve into a moral and legal force.

Most agencies of the United Nations report to the General Assembly. This is true of the Trusteeship Council and the Economic and Social Council, and through the latter all the Specialized Agencies are, in a sense, responsible to it. The Peace Observation Commission and the Collective Measures Committee, as well as the International Atomic Energy Agency are responsible to it. Undoubtedly, additional bodies created by the General Assembly will be attached to it. The smaller states will insist that the proposed disarmament agency be responsible to it as well as to the Security Council.

It might be wise if the General Assembly were in continuous session—that is, its major committees remaining in continuous session. At least two reasons would seem to dictate such a step. If Assembly sessions are too long, responsible statesmen cannot attend an adequate number of meetings. If there are serious problems before it, such as Korea, it may recess instead of adjourning, as in the Seventh and Eighth Assemblies, but without leaving peacemaking machinery in its absence. It might be that various committees of the General Assembly, particularly the First (the Political and Security Committee) could either be in continuous or semi-continuous session, leaving major decisions of the plenary body to be taken in a shorter period of time.

Some of the problems with which the Assembly deals cannot be finally dealt with in one particular plenary meeting. Their solution needs continuous machinery, which is not to be found in the Security Council or the Economic and Social Council. Several standing committees of the General Assembly are technically in continuous session, such as the committee dealing with the independence of colonial peoples.

Observers frequently point out a seeming duplication in United Nations debates. The Second and Third Committees of the General Assembly discuss over and over again problems that have been before the Economic and Social Council. The Third Committee of the General Assembly is engaged in a long debate over clauses of the human rights covenants that have already run the gamut of the Human Rights Commission. This duplication of debate seems inevitable until the principles of economic and social cooperation have been more fully developed and more clearly defined.

The fundamental problem of balancing the principle of the sovereign equality of states with centers of power will outlast the issue as it is resolved by the Committee of Thirty-Three on peacekeeping and financing. There are those who advocate a system of weighted voting in the General Assembly. Many ingenious plans for some such system in the General Assembly have been put forward. None seems acceptable. Certainly weighted voting cannot be based on wealth and resources. Man would hate to establish between nations the property qualifications that after a long struggle he discarded for the domestic franchise. Weighted voting could scarcely be based on any arbitrary standards, such as literacy. The nation with one of the highest standards of literacy in Europe, Germany, has been chiefly responsible for two world wars in the one generation. If representation were based on population without a ceiling, China and India would account for nearly half the votes in the General Assembly.

Two proposals for weighted voting involve, in a sense, creating an upper and lower house. It has been suggested that a fundamental reform of the Security Council make it, in a sense, the "upper house" of a legislative body composed of the Security Council and the General Assembly. Another suggestion has been made that the General Assembly sit twice in acting as a legislative body. In one sitting, it would accord one vote to each state irrespective of size. In another sitting, it would accord plural votes according to population up to a fixed figure. Legislation would pass both "houses," so to speak.

Various types of weighted voting have been developed in the Specialized Agencies of the United Nations.

A type of weighted voting in the problem of peacekeeping may be worked out by the committee appointed by the Nineteenth General Assembly to consider the future of peacekeeping and its financing. A previous chapter points out that in assessing the dues for peacekeeping in the Congo, the General Assembly divided its membership into two groups: the twenty-six developed countries, and the balance comprising the developing countries. The former took over a portion of the assessments of the latter.

Altogether new and anticipated compromises may be found between the rigidity of the five-Great-Power veto in the Security Council and the rigidity of one vote per state in the General Assembly—that is, if the statesmen keep their heads and the East-West and North-South conflicts do not prevail.

By the Development of the Processes to Create World Law and for Greater
Use of the International Court of Justice

These questions arise: Does the United Nations need more comprehensive machinery to make law? Shall it be centered on the General Assembly? Each chapter of this book has provided illustrations of the manifold ways in which the United Nations has added to world law. The General Assembly has acted as a legislative body. Certain of its resolutions through wide acceptance have become "recognized as laying down rules binding on states." The United Nations organization itself, by the decision of the General Assembly, has functioned as a government in Libya, West Irian, and elsewhere.

In developing a variety of means for the settlement of unexpected disputes, the bodies of the United Nations have added to common law. Regulations of the Specialized Agencies governing world health standards and atomic safeguards become binding on many states. It had to be so. A world of atomic energy, outer space exploration, and revolution of underdeveloped dependent peoples necessitates the development of world law, or otherwise mankind might well be destroyed.

The question arises, Does the United Nations need a more orderly legislative procedure in the General Assembly?—or, putting it popularly, When can the General Assembly pass laws? One may assume that the Specialized Agencies will continue to add international regulations or laws in their respective fields. The legislative authority of the General Assembly then would be primarily, but not exclusively, for the maintenance of peace. The conclusion cannot be escaped that under conditions of modern life growing ever more complex, the General Assembly must function as a legislative body to produce world law. Here the question of the reform of the General Assembly and weighted voting must be reconsidered.

The imagination might project the expansion of the United Nations far into the future to ask if, when, and where the breakthrough will occur so the international system can deal with the individual in crimes against the peace and in the protection of human rights. The most drastic was contained in the Baruch report when the United States proposed that the Atomic Energy Commission could punish the individual or the nation guilty of violating the Atomic Energy Agreement.

By Revision of the Text of the Charter

The question of a review conference to consider revising the Charter has arisen repeatedly in the last ten years. Each time the matter has been deferred. The small states were unhappy at San Francisco with the authority given the five Great Powers in the Security Council. As a consequence, the Great Powers made two concessions to the smaller states. They took a pledge that the veto would be used sparingly, which, of course, the Soviet Union has not respected. They provided that the question of a Charter Review Conference would automatically be placed on the agenda of the Tenth General Assembly. If such a conference had not already been held, the Tenth General Assembly could call a review conference by a simple majority.

At the Tenth Assembly there were such overshadowing problems that there was little sentiment among members to hold a review conference. Consequently, the Assembly decided to take advantage of the appropriate clause of the Charter and called a review conference in principle, but left to the Twelfth Assembly the determination of the date for such a conference. Again it has been deferred.

There has been considerable agitation in the United States and in other Western powers for a review conference. In preparation for the possibility that the Tenth General Assembly would call such a conference, the Department of State conducted hearings throughout the country as to what kind of changes in the Charter or in the structure of the organization witnesses would recommend. It was more of an educational than a fact-finding effort.

It would seem that the time for Charter review has not yet arrived.

It is the history of constitutions that in a moment of idealism and crisis people adopt a rule of conduct that may be difficult for them to live up to when the heroic mood passes. Then they are forced to follow rules of conduct that they would not adopt if they were to write their constitutions at that time. This is the history of the United Nations Charter. The time for its review is in another moment of idealism and crisis, when the basic document can be revised to be stronger than the original. That time has not yet come. The nations have not yet matched the idealism of 1945. Many have been afraid of Charter review up to now for the reason that revision might result in a retreat from the obligations written into the Charter in 1945.

If a review conference were to be held at the present time, the Soviet Union would undoubtedly make an effort to reduce the power of the Secretary-General, substituting "troika." It would further try to reduce the authority of the General Assembly and turn the clock back to the Security Council with its Great-Power veto. And undoubtedly the colonial powers, still smarting under the position that the United Nations has taken for the liquidation of colonial empires, would make an effort to strengthen Article 2, Paragraph 7, providing that the United Nations shall not intervene in matters essentially of domestic concern.

And the United States has not made up its mind as to how strong it wants the United Nations to become.

The foregoing paragraphs expressed the author's view before the crisis over peacekeeping and financing hit the Nineteenth General Assembly. It could well be that this crisis and a fear of the members that the United Nations might be seriously weakened would create the mood to make revisions of the Charter to strengthen the organization.

However, it may be that through a process of agreement among the members important reforms to strengthen the organization could be made. The Great Powers might agree to such reforms when they would not give unanimous agreement for revision of the actual text of the Charter. It has been seen how widely the powers of the United Nations have shifted and grown through consensus and a liberal interpretation of the Charter.

It may well be that the dramatic strengthening of the organization may come through the effort to achieve total disarmament. In 1955 the nations shied away from a review of the Charter because they lacked a challenge in the light of which the Charter could be strengthened. The movement for general and complete disarmament under international control may provide this challenge. However, revision may never be accomplished through a review conference as contemplated in Article 109 of the Charter. It is possible that, having decided upon the strengthened security machinery necessary for general and complete disarmament, the nations will graft this machinery on the United Nations or revise the Charter to meet this plan, under the regular amendment procedure.

Means of strengthening the United Nations and revising its covenant are secondary to the attitude of the members. This is the subject of the next chapter.

IX

ATTITUDE OF MEMBERS

"I have now said everything I have to say on the subject." Thus Dag Hammarskjöld described the Introduction to his Annual Report to the Sixteenth General Assembly. He was talking to Andrew Cordier as he was about to board the plane for his final trip to the Congo. Two days later his broken body was found in the plane wreckage in Rhodesia.

In this Introduction, Mr. Hammarskjöld wrote:

> On the one side, it has in various ways become clear that certain members conceive of the Organization as a static conference machinery for resolving conflicts of interest and ideologies with a view to peaceful coexistence, within the Charter, to be served by a Secretariat which is to be regarded not as fully internationalized but as representing within its ranks those very interests and ideologies.
>
> Other Members have made it clear that they conceive of the Organization primarily as a dynamic instrument of governments through which they, jointly and for the same purpose, should seek such reconciliation but through which they should also try to develop forms of executive action, undertaken on behalf of all Members, and aiming at forestalling conflicts and resolving them, once they have arisen, by appropriate diplomatic or political means, in a spirit of objectivity and

in implementation of the principles and purposes of
the Charter.

Some saw in the remarks of the Secretary-General a
premonition of death. Others interpreted his statement as
meaning that he had written such a good report that he did
not see how he could ever improve on it. It was undoubtedly
different from the average report of the Secretary-General to
the General Assembly. Instead of containing the over-all
annual review of the work of the organization, it was an ex-
pression of his basic philosophy on the nature of the United
Nations itself and the poignant dilemma posed by the basic
viewpoints about the United Nations.

The Secretary-General saw a comparison between the development of ethics within a nation and within the international community. He said:

> Together, these parts of the Charter lay down some
> basic rules of international ethics by which all Member
> States have committed themselves to be guided. To a
> large extent, the rules reflect standards accepted as
> binding for life within States. Thus, they appear, in the
> main, as a projection into the international arena and
> the international community of purposes and princi-
> ples already accepted as being of national validity. In
> this sense, the Charter takes a first step in the direc-
> tion of an organized international community, and this
> independently of the organs set up for international
> cooperation. Due to different traditions, the state of
> social development and the character of national in-
> stitutions, wide variations naturally exist as to the
> application in national life of the principles reflected
> in the Charter, but it is not too difficult to recognize
> the common elements behind those differences. It is
> therefore not surprising that such principles of na-
> tional application could be transposed into an agreed
> basis also for international behavior and cooperation.

At the moment when nations are very much worried about the capacity of some of the very new members to adjust themselves to these principles, the late Secretary-General's words are wise and comforting.

Dag Hammarskjöld went on to define the five fundamental principles to be found in the Charter: (1) a system of equal political rights, (2) equal economic rights, (3) the rule of law, (4) outlawing the use of armed force save in the common defense, and (5) adjustment or settlement of international disputes or situations which might lead to a breach of the peace.

Obviously, Mr. Hammarskjöld concluded that the dynamic international society, which he believed the Charter contemplated, could not be squared with the view that the United Nations was simply a conference mechanism to achieve coexistence between ideological blocs.

Putting it another way, the fundamental question concerning the attitude of the members toward the United Nations today can be stated in the following terms: Is the United Nations the foundation of international policy? Or is it an instrument that nations can use or reject as shortsighted self-interest dictates?

Any review of how the United Nations has functioned must take into consideration the attitude of its members. After almost two decades many members have not made up their minds how strong they want the United Nations to be. In fact, they have not made up their minds what they want the United Nations to be. They have not made up their minds how much supranational authority they wish it to have. They have not determined how far they wish to go in developing the world organization into a growing, dynamic, international society serving nations, and indeed individuals, as a government does in a domestic community—bringing people together in a civilized way of life based on law.

Use of the United Nations to deal with great political and economic problems has ebbed and flowed like the tide. There have been moments of great use and of sad neglect. Sometimes the lights have burned all night as the Security Council or the General Assembly met around the clock to prevent war. There have been other times when nations have felt it to their advantage to take the law into their own hands.

At a given moment, the situation may be discouraging. The twentieth year of the United Nations, which had been proclaimed by the Eighteenth General Assembly as International Cooperation Year, opened with the Assembly unable to vote because of the deadlock over paying for peacekeeping operations, and with Indonesia's withdrawal from the United Nations. However, a review of twenty years would indicate such a rapid growth of the United Nations, such a rapid increase in its membership, such a wide acceptance of a variety of obligations that one may conclude that, instinctively and driven by the law of necessity, the nations have been moving to create a dynamic international society.

The Charter was drafted when the world was at war. The peoples of many nations were then serving together and making terrible sacrifices to win that war. They believed that with peace would come an international society strong enough to prevent war and to build a just international order.

If these hopes dim as the memory of the war recedes and the nations treat the United Nations as an instrument of policy, a diplomatic tool to be used as a matter of convenience and an organ of propaganda, the organization will tend to become an instrument of governments, not of peoples. The foreign offices, and frequently the more timid members of such foreign offices, will determine at any moment what instrument shall be used to carry out their policies. When increasingly storms come, there will be grave danger that the United Nations will be bypassed because men of little imagination would lack the policies and the boldness necessary for success through the United Nations. These men would fall back on old ways of meeting grave world problems, even though these methods have given man the major failures of the twentieth century.

The members of the United Nations, as has been said earlier in these chapters, come from very different backgrounds. Some have thousands of years of history. They have contributed much to the religion, philosophy, and civilization of the world. Others are quite new and have just emerged from the tribal state. Some are rich; some are poor; some have small lands and a densely concentrated population; others have virgin lands to develop.

Naturally, each member's attitude toward the United Nations is influenced by what that member is most anxious to derive from it. But since each one's desires can only be achieved in terms of the common good of all, common standards arise that are part of the dynamic system of which we speak. It is what Dag Hammarskjöld meant when, in speaking of the different backgrounds of nations, he said that it was not too difficult to recognize the common intentions behind those differences; nor is it surprising that such principles of national application "could be transposed into an agreed basis . . . for international behavior and cooperation."

If this is so, what is required of the statesmen and of the peoples they represent to build the international community? One is inclined to speak of statesmen and peoples interchangeably, because at United Nations meetings one usually judges a people by the statesmen who speak for them. As one watches the statesmen as they speak and vote in United Nations meetings, one recognizes that they reflect the point of view and the degree of sophistication of their own people. Frequently this leadership plays a part in determining the point of view of their respective countries in the United Nations. Thus Iran, led by Entezam, the Philippines, by Romulo, and Pakistan, by Sir Zafrulla Kahn, may play a stronger role than they would with less able leadership.

It would seem that among the qualities of statesmanship and national capacity needed to develop the international community are some characteristics fairly common among individuals in a domestic community.

The statesmen and the peoples they represent must be able to see the difference between self-interest and common interest. The former might be sheer selfishness by which the member would be willing to destroy the international community for immediate self-interest. Understanding of the latter means that in the long run the nation's self-interest is advanced through the common good and not by running contrary to it.

People must have the capacity not only to see the other nation's point of view but to appreciate it and to respect it. Simply to see another's point of view might mean being better armed to oppose it; appreciating it and respecting it makes an honorable agreement possible without appeasement.

Statesmen must have a feeling of responsibility to the entire world community. They must develop that capacity, such as has been developed over a long period of time in national legislatures, to represent the entire community as well as their own constituencies. Indeed, this sophisticated statesman must be capable of self-criticism; capable of recognizing a mistake; capable of a sense of humor. Without these there may develop a lack of proportion that can be terrible in its consequences.

Thousands of speeches have been made in United Nations bodies. The brilliant ones are made in the General Assembly, where statesmen may seem to vie with each other not only in putting forward their countries' interests but also in discussing the problems confronting the United Nations itself. Sometimes they are very critical of it and of each other. But there are times when an outstanding speech is made that shows a perception and over-all understanding of the problems of the world and their possible solution. Such a speech may be a very comforting as well as an inspiring one, for it puts problems in historical perspective. Such a speech may frequently be made by a statesman from one of the smallest powers.

Neither size nor wealth are automatic criteria of sophistication, or of the awareness of the obligations of community life. Two of the smallest states of the Middle East, possibly the two most deficient in natural resources, Tunisia and Israel, are the most sophisticated. Occasionally in the United Nations General Assembly a speech is delivered that is outstanding among so many speeches that are only reflections of national points of view. Abba Eban, of Israel, delivered such a speech during the opening days of the Nineteenth General Assembly, an Assembly that had not been able to organize itself because of the dispute over the payment of assessments. He said, in part:

> This strong world-wide emphasis on the pacific settlement of disputes is not only a reaction to the nuclear peril. It is inspired by hope as well as by fear. The world is moving away from the bi-polar confrontation of East and West during the 40's and 50's towards a new international order marked by diversity, pluralism, variety, freedom and dissent. It is not an age for crusades. In great-power relations the keywords are "coexistence" and "co-operation." And in small nations, life has to be lived on two levels: on the intimate level of national distinctiveness—and in the broader arena of intense international co-operation. In economic and

social relationships the trend is no longer towards dog-
matic extremes of exclusive private ownership or exclusive public control. Most of our societies are mixed
societies in which private initiative and State planning
exist together within a single economic framework. In
philosophy and religion there is a search for unifying
common principles, not for divisive barriers. It prom-
ises to be the age of tolerance. It is the ecumenical
age. . . .

Four Great Powers—the United States, the United Kingdom, the Soviet Union, and France, together with Nationalist
China—were given permanent seats on the Security Council and the right of veto, because it was felt that they were in
a position to make an exceptional contribution to the maintenance of international peace and security.

One might add to these five Great Powers a few others,
such as Italy and Japan.

The above nations might labor under the delusion that
they have power enough to go it alone without the United
Nations. They have participated in the long history of power
politics. They could argue that they do not need the protection of the United Nations. They could say, therefore, that it
is not incumbent on them to make a special contribution to
its development. But in an age of possible nuclear warfare
and the conquest of outer space, it is an illusion for them to
believe that they can be secure outside the law of the world
community and without the cooperation of the other members of the human family.

As for Great Britain, she is one of the most understanding
members. She seems to have exhibited the same inconsistent
support as has the Government of the United States—
sometimes making important contributions and at other
times neglecting the United Nations. Certainly the votes in
the General Assembly and the Security Council would indi-

cate that Great Britain usually votes on the side of construc-
tive action. As might be expected, she supported the action in
Korea and was the second largest contributor of forces to the
United Nations army resisting aggression there.

British public opinion, first in support of the League of
Nations, and then of the United Nations, has been more
vocal than in most countries. A large section of the British
people supported the United Nations against their own government when the latter invaded Suez in 1956. One wonders
in how many countries the United Nations Association
would have had the courage and in fact the liberty of choice
that the British Association expressed in support of the
United Nations against its own government in the Suez crisis.

At the present time, the British attitude toward the United
Nations is materially affected by the revolt against colonialism and the demand of the new states in the United Nations
for the independence of every part of the British Empire.
There have been startling developments since Winston
Churchill said that he had not become His Majesty's representative to liquidate the British Empire. Rapidly Britain has
been advancing her colonies toward self-government and
then independence. The majority of them have elected to
remain members of the British Commonwealth.

Nevertheless, it was to be expected that the British would
feel that the General Assembly had violated the limits of the
Charter in pushing so vigorously for independence of colonial areas. The British did not give warm support to the
program of the United Nations in the Congo. At times the
British Government is caught in the conflict between members of the Commonwealth, such as that of India and Pakistan over Kashmir.

Many supporters of the United Nations in the United
Kingdom believe that the Tory government relegated the
United Nations to second place in its diplomatic considera-

tions, frequently forgetting about it. It is ironical that Sir Hugh Foot, who resigned as His Majesty's representative on the Trusteeship Council because he disagreed with the conservatism of British colonial policy, should now, under the Labor government, as Lord Caradon, be head of the British Mission to the United Nations. His position in the cabinet is enhanced by his having been made Minister of State for Foreign Affairs.

At the moment, France is a tragic disappointment to those who remember that country's support of the principles of the world community in previous days. Between the First and Second World Wars, France was one of the strongest advocates of collective security at the League of Nations. Hers was one of the most fertile minds at Geneva. A statesman at Geneva remarked to the author in the twenties that when a problem was before the League of Nations there would usually be two plans advanced for solution—the draft prepared by the Secretariat and the draft submitted by the French delegates. And it was the great orator of the League of Nations, Aristide Briand, who coined the famous statement: "There is not one peace for America, not one peace for Asia, not one peace for Europe, one peace for Africa, but only one peace for the entire world." He was the first advocate of the United States of Europe within the framework of the League of Nations.

The French delegates played a fairly important role in drafting the Charter at San Francisco. Indeed, these statesmen carried forward France's tradition of a world society in the early days of the United Nations.

However, French policy at first was less concerned with the over-all community than with the development of the European community. With the memory of a humiliating occupation and anxious for the restoration of French prestige, as well as resentful of United Nations debates on Algeria, President de Gaulle reduced France's role in the United Nations. To those who remember the days of Aristide Briand, Paul Boncour, and Albert Thomas, it is almost heartbreaking to see the French delegates play a negligible role in United Nations affairs. It is hard to imagine the delegates of France abstaining on an important moral issue. Referring again to these great statesmen, it would almost seem as though the decline in French oratory coincides with their decreasing interest in the United Nations.

It is the Soviet Union, more than any other Great Power, which has maintained a position of fixed rigidity in the political work of the United Nations, and frequently a position of obstructionism in its other activities. In practically all areas there has been that hard rock, that fixed position, that unwillingness to compromise, to negotiate—only willingness to veto or abstain. For some years there has been a solid bloc of Communist states which have not been permitted to exercise choice or objectivity in their United Nations votes. The satellite states in Eastern Europe are showing greater economic and political independence—the monolith is disintegrating. Obviously such independence would be expressed last in the United Nations. Nevertheless, a slight restlessness on their part can be found in United Nations meetings.

The Soviet Government continues to believe in the dictatorship of the four great "policemen" in the United Nations. That government's use of the veto in the Security Council indicates that it intends that this dictatorship function according to its wishes. Almost everything that the General Assembly has done at the expense of the Security Council, the Soviet Union considers illegal.

Much of the frustration of the United Nations can be blamed on the Soviet Union because of its use of the veto in the Security Council and because of its insistence on extending the veto to finance and disarmament. It is only fair to point out, however, that in the early days of the cold war the Western states, including the United States, forced a vote in the General Assembly when such a vote was not necessary for the preservation of peace. The desire seemed to be to register overwhelming majorities against the Soviet Union.

The writer remembers Jan Masaryk's last service as a Czech delegate to the United Nations General Assembly before he was to return to Prague and his martyrdom. It was outside the Political Committee room, in which the Soviet and the United States representatives were denouncing each other's countries in the bitterest terms. Masaryk turned to some of his friends, including the author, shook his head sadly, and said, "If they only realized what they were doing."

Having failed to maintain a dominant position in the Security Council by the veto and feeling itself outvoted in the General Assembly, the Soviet Union turned first to the device of parity and then an insistence on "troika." In 1960, in demanding the resignation of Dag Hammarskjöld, the Soviet Union advocated "troika." However, after Hammarskjöld's death in 1961 U Thant was elected Acting Secretary-General and in 1962 Secretary-General without any move in the direction of "troika." Much less is said of this idea at the present time, presumably because of the overwhelming opposition of most of the non-Communist members.

If the author seems to devote more attention to the attitude of the United States, it is because this book is written from the American point of view. The policy of the United States toward the United Nations has vibrated between the highest idealism and calculated neglect. It is a record both of careful planning and improvisation.

Positive Role of the United States

On the plus side, the United States has been in a position to do more for the United Nations than any other Great Power, and it has done so. The American people were happy to have a few acres in the heart of their most populous city contributed as international territory for the capital of the United Nations. The United States has been the largest single contributor to United Nations budgets, both regular and voluntary, and to special assessments for peacekeeping. It takes the leading place in United Nations emergency projects.

At the time when the United States was the sole possessor of the atomic bomb it offered to scrap its atomic program, and therefore its considerable military advantage, in return for adequate inspection and control. It made most advanced suggestions for a supranational United Nations authority in a specific area when it suggested that an international commission be empowered to punish the nation or the individual violating atomic agreements. And this without the right of Great-Power veto!

The United States has contributed much toward the evolution of the United Nations. It suggested the Uniting for Peace Resolution, which shifted the center of gravity from the Security Council to the General Assembly. It was the first to suggest that the Collective Measures Committee make a study of a United Nations Legion. The Point Four Program of President Truman inspired the Expanded United Nations Technical Assistance Program. The United States Government has had much to do with the Declaration of Human Rights.

It was the United States that challenged the United Nations to meet aggression at the 38th Parallel in Korea. This country contributed the greatest number of troops and suffered thousands of casualties in support of this effort. The late President of the United States John F. Kennedy said at the Sixteenth General Assembly that the Assembly should declare that the United Nations Charter be extended ". . . to the limits of man's exploration in the universe." He projected the United Nations Decade of Development.

Of the Great Powers, the United States gave the United Nations the strongest support in its peacekeeping program in the Congo. It contributed 50 per cent of the cost of that program.

No more dramatic challenge has ever been made to the United Nations than that contained in President Eisenhower's "Atoms for Peace" speech.

Negative Role of the United States

One could begin the minus side of the ledger by referring to what happened to delay implementing this speeech of President Eisenhower. Chapter VII describes in some detail the establishment of the International Atomic Energy Agency (IAEA) and its high purposes. However, there occurred a period of four years' neglect before the announcement in 1963 by the Chairman of the United States Atomic Energy Commission that this country had made a policy decision to negotiate for the transfer of its "bilateral safeguards responsibility to the Agency."

American policy in the United Nations sometimes gives the impression of improvisation with the lack of a carefully thought-out policy to reap the fruits of a good position. In 1956, the United States was the only Great Power with membership on the Security Council willing to oppose use of armed force in violation of the Charter from whatever source. It was willing that the Charter be invoked against the British, French, and Israeli in Suez and the Soviet Union in Hungary.

Never has the prestige of the United States in the United Nations been higher. One would have expected that the United States Government would have followed its advantage in the General Assembly by demanding constructive solutions of outstanding problems, particularly in the Middle

East. Indeed, the American representative introduced a draft resolution looking toward some constructive solutions. In the face of opposition, the draft was not pressed. But it would seem that the United States was in a sufficiently good position to insist, to insist, and insist again on progressive measures. Such insistence would have given the United States the offensive in the Assembly in demanding a fresh approach to some issues that had dragged on altogether too long.

Instead, to the consternation of almost everyone and the dismay of the smaller states, the play was suddenly taken away from the American Delegation in the General Assembly and the game was played out in Washington. Suddenly, the Secretary of State announced the "Eisenhower Doctrine." Congress was asked to give the President authority to employ the armed forces of the United States to secure and protect the territorial and political independence of any nation in the Middle East requesting such aid against overt armed aggression by international communism.

The author of this book appeared before the Senate and House foreign relations committees to urge that nothing be done to bypass the United Nations or to weaken the American position in the organization at the moment when American prestige was at its very highest.

The various warnings were not followed. The "Eisenhower Doctrine" was announced; it was given the most cursory relationship to the United Nations. And so, at the moment of victory in upholding the principles of the Charter in the Middle East, the United States bypassed the United Nations to announce a unilateral security role in the Middle East.

Foreign policy for a Great Power under modern conditions is a highly complex process. It is not limited to ambassadors sent to friendly capitals by the foreign office. Diplomacy today involves participation in the complex system of international relationships from the maintenance of international health standards through intellectual cooperation. All agencies of the government are concerned with international relations.

Consequently, one department of a government can be deeply committed to conducting its contact with the rest of the world in harmony with the principles of the Charter and as much as possible through its machinery. But to some other government officials the United Nations might seem to be a nuisance, getting in the way of their quick and possibly shortsighted bilateral or unilateral approach to a problem. Consequently, when the head of the United States Mission to the United Nations is given Cabinet rank and when the head of the British Mission to the United Nations is made a minister of state, it is felt that these men are in a better position to uphold their countries' obligations to the United Nations in the jungle of governmental policy-forming.

The United States, as the twentieth year of the United Nations opens, is engaged in large-scale military activities in Vietnam. It is constantly urged to extend the war northward, with a possible repetition of the catastrophe that followed General MacArthur's march to the Yalu River in the Korean conflict. The time seemed to have arrived some years ago when the United States should have asked the United Nations for help in meeting the problem of the three states of Indochina. It can be replied that the United Nations is handicapped in dealing with this problem because the Communist Chinese delegates are not seated in the United Nations. One need not abandon one's detestation for the conduct of the Chinese Communist Government by saying that the United States, by refusing to recognize the entire problem and to be less rigid-minded on the question of Communist China, must bear a responsibility for what has happened.

Shortsighted military considerations may at times run contrary to a statesman's pledge to the United Nations. Explosion by the military of a nuclear bomb in outer space is recognized by most everyone as contrary to the statement that President Kennedy had made to the General Assembly a few months earlier, in which he said that we must keep the cold war out of the colder reaches of outer space.

Four Presidents of the United States have clearly indicated their support of the United Nations as a foundation of American foreign policy. Much of the growth of the United Nations has been due to American inspiration and participation. The Bureau of International Organization Affairs in the Department of State enjoys the confidence of the Secretary of State and the President. The United States has been represented by able heads of Mission and devoted members of the Mission.

Overwhelming public opinion must support the United States Government in continuing to give leadership to the United Nations. It must constantly be alert to any trend to neglect or bypass it.

Another group of nations would contain the old-line middle powers. Here one thinks to a considerable extent of the nations of Northern and Western Europe and the members of the British Commonwealth. They are states in the main with a traditional experience in international relations. They have a considerable sophistication in world politics. They represent many of the ideas and hopes of the League of Nations.

In this group, the Scandinavian countries, the Low Countries, and some members of the British Commonwealth, particularly Canada, have shown at times an exceptional singlemindedness in their willingness to support high principles in the United Nations with positive action. The role of Canada has been one of the most outstanding. Her power position is unique. Canada is a member of the British Commonwealth and shares three thousand miles of unfortified border with the United States. She shares the western frontier without having participated in the excess of pioneer isolationism of the United States. She shares the traditions of the British Empire without participating in a spirit of colonialism. It was the Canadian delegate who found a formula for breaking the deadlock which was keeping many states out of the United Nations. The Canadian Minister for External Affairs, Lester B. Pearson, in the debates over Suez suggested a United Nations Emergency Force. The suggestion was instantly supported by the representative of the United States, Ambassador Henry Cabot Lodge.

The Netherlands and Belgium have shared the disillusionment of the colonial powers over the support which the United Nations gave to independence for the Dutch territories in Asia and the Belgian territories in Africa.

Several of these nations make a greater per capita contribution to United Nations technical assistance than the United States or any other large power.

It may not be wholly accurate to group the Latin American states in one category. They have not always voted together. But in the main they have stood for certain identical principles. They have made an important contribution in upholding the principles of justice and equity. It is to be expected that the Latin American members would contribute much to any strengthening of the rule of law and a broader role for the World Court. But, unfortunately, their idealism is frequently not matched by financial or other material contributions to such United Nations emergency efforts as UNEF, expanded technical assistance, or the problem of refugees.

The Latin American states are in a unique position. They are members of the oldest and most clearly developed regional organization, the Organization of American States, which has been brought closely within the framework of the United Nations. This advantageous position enables them to ask for and secure two seats on the Security Council, three seats on the Economic and Social Council, and two judge-ships on the World Court. This is, in fact, a much stronger representation in United Nations bodies than Asian or African states enjoy.

As the membership of the United Nations increases through the breakup of the colonial empires, there are more and more underdeveloped states. Their role in the United Nations, the blessing that they bring to the organization, and the difficulties that they present to it are discussed in Chapter VI. One cannot lump these states together in many categories of problems. They have very different historical backgrounds and cultures. Some have a strong tie to the West, others try to revolt against everything Western. The difference between many of them, both geographically and culturally, is as different as their division with the Western world. Frequently one hears the announcement in United Nations meetings that the African states or the Asian states or the Asian-African states will meet at such and such a time. They do not agree on a wide range of subjects. Their greatest unity is expressed against colonialism—sometimes it seems almost unreasoning.

As Walter Reuther wrote in a paper prepared for the 19th Assembly of the World Federation of United Nations Associations held in New Delhi in January, 1965:

> The phase of "independence," in short, is now ending. Almost three-fourths of United Nations member states today—83 out of 115—are nations of the "developing South," in Asia, Africa and Latin America. The dominant problem today is no longer the achievement of independence for aspiring peoples but the working out of the terms of *interdependence*, in a world in which no nation and no people, however powerful, can survive and prosper in a vacuum.

Earlier in this chapter it was said that the United Nations must be the foundation of foreign policy rather than an instrument of diplomatic choice. Possibly a stronger phrase could be used. The problem is one of moral standards. There are those in other countries and in the United States who say that there can be no morality in international relations; that a government's first concern is to defend the interests of its people by any means available. Such a concept would continue all the diplomatic and military practices of the past that led the world to the brink of destruction twice in this century. The success of the United Nations is finally dependent on the nations believing and practicing in international relations the same standard of conduct that they consider the only standard upon which a domestic community can be based.

How has the United Nations done in its twenty years of history? The contrasts are startling. In some ways it is weak. Its budget is insignificant. Its most devoted followers will bypass it in critical situations. It must stand paralyzed at the Nineteenth General Assembly in fear of a confrontation between two great states that by fortune and atomic power have altogether too much influence in comparison with the rest of the members of the human family.

On the other hand, it has withstood the development of atomic energy and mobilized public opinion both for its control and its peaceful use. It has gradually developed law among nations and dared to extend the law of the Charter into the area of man's exploration of outer space. It has helped a great part of the world to freedom and to adjust itself to the world community. It, and its numerous family, have launched a vast program of economic and social advancement. It has prevented wars.

The author shares the view of millions of others that it is imperative that the United Nations succeed in the objectives outlined in the first chapter of this book.

One wonders what the world will be like ten years from now—twenty—fifty. Brave explorers and air-cargoes will be making the journey into outer space. Atomic energy will have more nearly supplanted the diminishing sources of conventional energy. The population of the world will have so fantastically increased that it will have doubled by the end of the century. Disarmament may be a fact. Areas of human misery will have vanished.

At the same time, there will undoubtedly be larger and larger political and economic units. One can see Western Europe developing very rapidly into an economic United States of Europe. Africa south of the Sahara, a widely diversified and tremendous area, with a small population, may surprisingly see several large federations. As the population increases, vast areas of the world may tend to federate, and the number of member nations and the number of delegates to the United Nations might actually decrease.

Under any circumstances, there will be more need than ever for the over-all world organization, the over-all world law, and authority. If man is to have peace, the United Nations obviously will adjust itself to these vast changes and will influence them even more decisively than it has in the past.